The Irish Bull God

Marie-Louise von Franz, Honorary Patron
Studies in Jungian Psychology
by Jungian Analysts
Daryl Sharp, General Editor

The Irish Bull God

Image of Multiform and Integral Masculinity

SYLVIA BRINTON PERERA

Sylvia Brinton Perera is the author of two other books
in this series: *Descent to the Goddess: A Way of Initiation
for Women* (1981) and *The Scapegoat Complex: Toward
a Mythology of Shadow and Guilt* (1986).

National Library of Canada Cataloguing in Publication

Perera, Sylvia Brinton
　　The Irish bull god: image of integrated masculinity /
　　Sylvia Brinton Perera

(Studies in Jungian psychology by Jungian analysts; no. 107)

Includes bibliographical references and index.

ISBN 1-894574-08-7

1. Masculinity.
2. Dagda (Celtic deity).
3. Archetype (Psychology).
I. Title. II. Series.

BL980.I7P47 2004　　　　155.3'32　　　C2003-902432-6

INNER CITY BOOKS
Box 1271, Station Q, Toronto, ON M4T 2P4, Canada

Telephone (416) 927-0355 / FAX (416) 924-1814
Web site: www.innercitybooks.net / E-mail: admin@innercitybooks.net

Honorary Patron: Marie-Louise von Franz.
Publisher and General Editor: Daryl Sharp.
Senior Editor: Victoria Cowan.

INNER CITY BOOKS was founded in 1980 to promote the
understanding and practical application of the work of C.G. Jung.

Cover: "The Dagda," wood carving by Michael Quirke.

Printed and bound in Canada by University of Toronto Press Incorporated

CONTENTS

See final pages for Catalogue of other Inner City titles

Acknowledgments

For their helpful comments about this material, I want to thank the participants at Jungian conferences in Washington, DC; New York City; Los Angeles; Assisi, Italy; and at the Friends Conference on Religion and Psychology in Anneville, PA. Members of several study groups in Ireland have also heard parts of this material and responded generously. Especially, I am grateful to my friends Martin Byrne, Georgette Kelley, Suzi Naiburg, Michael Paull, Mary Rentschler, Cathie Ryan, Mark Seides, Susan Shaughnessy, Gertrud Ujhely, and the late E. Christopher Whitmont who have given me their support and astute reactions. Michael Quirke, woodcarver and storyteller in Sligo, Ireland, created the modern shape-shifting figure of the Dagda used here on the cover.

It goes without saying how much I have learned from the authors of works cited in the bibliography, as well as others too numerous to mention. I have learned, too, from the analysts-in-training who took the courses on Celtic Symbolism in Clinical Practice that I have taught over the years. From interactions with clients in psychotherapy I have repeatedly seen the timeless relevance of the material. I have altered the clinical examples, used here with permission, and sometimes combined material to protect confidentiality. As will be clear, my purpose in relating clinical material is not to describe the intricate dance of psychotherapy itself, which I have done in other works, but to explore an image that I have come to value and want to share.

We shall not cease from exploration
And the end of all our exploring
Will be to arrive where we started
And know the place for the first time.
—T.S. Eliot, "Little Gidding."

Ancient forms propel the future.
—Emilie Conrad.[1]

The self is the total, timeless man, and as such corresponds to the original, spherical, bisexual being.
—C.G Jung, "The Psychology of the Transference."

---

[1] Founder of Continuum movement. From a workshop October 13, 2002, New York City.

1

Introduction

Pattern is the Living Being that is Forever existent.
—Plato, *Timaeus,* 37.

Within an eight-month period four years ago, I experienced a personal crisis—the deaths of my brother, father, former analyst, and life partner. I was left with a deep sense of loss of the important males in my life. At first I had no idea how to handle the emptiness and chaos that reverberated through me. The tender care of friends and family could go only so far. The hole felt limitless and unassuageable.

Of course, women the world over have faced such losses before. Sometimes, when the deaths are the result of war and political violence, women have banded together to witness the disappeared. And indeed, at this point in history many are faced with similar ruptures of stability. The massacres of 9/11, current conflicts in the Middle East, and the rituals of death and domination that are bringing them about have forced even the most naive bystanders to face a profound, collective crisis. We call the conflicts that have precipitated this crisis by many names: Jihad vs. MacWorld, terror vs. freedom, holy men vs. idolatry, the downtrodden poor vs. the selfish rich. However we identify the opposing forces, the whole globe is suffering the chaos and anguish of their conflicts.

There are no simple solutions. My pilgrimages to Ground Zero in the months following September 11, 2001, my work with survivors and the families and friends of those who did not survive, my sense of the horrors loosed and courage needed in clients and friends around the world during the past decades, all leave me with a profound awareness that many of the anchors of our old complaisance cannot hold. As William Butler Yeats has said, "The cere-

9

mony of innocence is drowned . . . [and a] rough beast, its hour come round at last, / Slouches towards Bethlehem to be born."[2] Ever since I read this poem in college, I have wondered: How could this be? What is waiting to be born out of anarchy and chaos? And how are we to meet it? The images of the poem are searing. The questions are painfully relevant. How can we reach for answers?

Currently, scientists using nonlinear concepts affirm that chaos in open, self-organizing systems is both unpredictable and potentially transformative. When repetitive and cyclic patterns are disrupted, bifurcation and conflict emerge. One aspect recedes and a new focus acts as a strange attractor of energy to support a fundamental, qualitative reformation with a new order. The underlying attractor governs the behavior of a complicated but orderly process of restructuring and self-organization.

However, when we personally experience the throes of a major psychological shift, we feel it as anything but orderly. Instead we find ourselves in the grip of a process that seems anarchic, catastrophic, frightening; in a word, monstrous. Nonetheless, that process may bring transformation. When we can endure the painful dislocation that we suffer at such times, we may survive the death of old patterns of identity to discover the previously unrecognized information around which new structures and meanings can coalesce. Since we go through these phases repeatedly as we develop through life, we may come to a deeper understanding of the process itself. This enables us to participate more consciously in our own transformation.

As Jung recognized, the symbols we encounter in our dreams and daily life are expressions of archetypal patterns that organize psyche and world. We know that the information encoded in such living symbols tells us about both human health and dis-ease, interpersonally in societies and intrapsychically in each of us. The symbolic forms also encode information that is relevant to healing tur-

---

[2] "The Second Coming," in A. Norman Jeffares, ed., *W.B. Yeats: Selected Poetry*, p. 100.

bulences in psyche.[3] As we consciously relate to them, we may find helpful orientation and insight into the chaos and discover the new, though still unfamiliar order toward which they and we are moving.

Having experienced many such passages through chaos in myself and my analytic clients, I have come to realize that part of my spiritual practice as an introvert and a Jungian involves suffering through the painful disorientations and staying as attentive as possible to the symbolic images that arise in dreams and outer events even while I am feeling buffeted. I have learned that human consciousness may then open toward the new order waiting to be born. We can discover its emerging coherence through the increasing resonance between hitherto chaotic sensations, emotions, images and thoughts. We can see that they gradually point toward an unfamiliar but increasingly integrated picture of reality that we could not acknowledge before. Finally we may learn that the deeper order coming into distressed consciousness is an expression of the archetypal pattern we now need to incarnate more fully.

Such personal and collective wounds can open doorways through which to encounter new transpersonal realms. In my recent anguish I tried to remain open in spite of the confusion and intense, often polarized emotions. I paid close attention to my dreams and relationships to inner and outer figures to find their organizing symbols.

While I have written about several images of wholeness in female form, this time I found myself drawn to explore a male figure from ancient Irish myth. Discovering him was an enormous relief, for his image could support a necessary reordering in my psyche. Working with this figure, I realized again that, for me, encountering the rightfully fitting image is like a homeopathic remedy. In homeopathy, each substance that becomes a remedy is first tested to find out what physical and mental effects repeated dosage can cause in

---

[3] See my books, *Descent to the Goddess, The Scapegoat Complex* and *Celtic Queen Maeve and Addiction,* as relevant respectively to depression, shame and guilt, and addictions.

healthy individuals. These symptoms become the base line of essential information about the remedy, a description of its wholeness pattern. When a particular person is dis-eased, the doctor seeks the remedy with a pattern that has the closest similarity to the totality of symptoms the patient is experiencing. The patient's taking in the energy and/or information of the potentized remedy substance can arouse the stressed and chaotic system to move toward a new balanced order—that is, toward healing.[4]

I discovered that the image of the Irish Dagda functioned as a remedy for me. It has helped me to move through inner and outer chaos. As I have delved into his stories, the Dagda has become a potent presence that speaks to my personal condition. His figure has given me structures from the archetypal dimension through which I can reconnect to the integrated masculine that my own brother, father, analyst and partner had carried for me over the years.

Because the figure in its rich complexity held such fascination, I recognized that I idealized it. I know that the idealization served to compensate for my personal sense of loss as well as my Western culture's dishonoring and dismemberment of much that the Dagda represents. Thus when I have spoken about this old Irish deity to others, both men and women have responded, urging me to bring him to a wider audience. Writing this book has helped me to rebalance my own passions and find inner access to the sources symbolized by the Dagda. It is my hope that his image will also help others by pointing to their dormant potentials for integration. He suggests something of what the masculine might become when we have outgrown our contemporary adolescence as "societ[ies] invigorated by constant, romanticized, heroic violence,"[5] greed and competition.

The mythological material about the Dagda comes from an ancient deposit that has been passed down and worked over through millennia of Irish culture in both oral and written sources. However,

---

[4] See Edward C. Whitmont, *The Alchemy of Healing: Psyche and Soma.*
[5] Ian Buruma and Avishai Margalit, "Occidentalism," p. 6.

rather than trying to assess it historically, I have allowed the images
and tales that have collected around this figure from Neolithic to
medieval and even relatively modern times to form their own pattern of wholeness. The process has revealed the workings of an archetypal field that has timeless psychological verity.

The contemporary material in this book comes from personal
experience, my own and that of friends and colleagues. I also gathered some of it over three decades of work with psychotherapy clients. Weaving this psychological material across the warp of early
Irish mythology, I have sought areas where the two strands intersect
to reveal an underlying archetypal pattern. I have discovered that
many aspects of the symbolic field are meaningful and illuminating
for modern psychological work. In the process of discovery, I have
also sought a psychologically true-enough model of integrated masculinity to arouse the general reader to wonder and curiosity. Repeatedly I have asked: What might the Dagda's image mean for us
today?

To introduce you to the remarkable figure known in Irish as *In
Daghda*, I will often follow an old Irish form of listing the god's
attributes before I elaborate them and seek their contemporary
meaning for us. Subsequently I will use a kind of Celtic interlace to
weave old stories with modern clinical material and personal reflections. As we circle around in the clusters of images, you will, I
hope, arrive at a feel for the whole. As you encounter each new image or story, I invite you to let yourself take a moment to breathe
deeply, relax and orient yourself through your personal experience
of similar material. Such musing can help you open and deepen
your consciousness in order to follow all the threads and find your
own meanings in them.

2

The Bull God

Like the rough beast of Yeats's poem, slouching to be born out of the "anarchy [that] is loosed upon the world,"[6] the Dagda is himself a beast, a very earthy bull with all of the primordial energies and fertility potential that make him lord of animals and the harvest. But he is also more. He is an Irish shapeshifter. Thus he appears also as a mighty warrior, rousing terror in his enemies. He is a potent lover and the respectful partner of three Great Goddesses. He is a just and generous king who can bear and contain the opposites and all that is dished out to him. He is a builder and musician, a wise magus from time immemorial. He is an image of the archetypal Anthropos, a 6,000-year-old, ever-living ancient.

Such fullness is wondrous and comforting. I began to see that his stories presented me with an image of integration, a masculine symbol of one configuration of wholeness. In other words, he is a representative of what Jung called the Self, a psychic organizing center with an archetypal urge toward unity.[7]

Many people today are seeking that sense of integration. Even as we have become more comfortable with the idea of our psychological plurality, we are also struggling to discover a meaningful and authentic sense of completeness. Holding both our many-sided variety and underlying unity together in consciousness is challenging and difficult. It requires accepting the experiences of a constantly shifting dynamism. For me it also requires trying to discover image patterns that can provide signposts to the intricate, numinous crossroads of the many and the one. Such symbols can orient us as we try to live consciously our intimations of the interweavings.

---

[6] "The Second Coming," in Jeffares, ed., *W.B. Yeats*, p. 99.
[7] See Edward C. Whitmont, *The Symbolic Quest: Basic Concepts of Analytical Psychology*, chap. 14.

The Irish Dagda offers an image of both multiplicity and integration that has provided me with orientation and psychological sustenance. I hope that readers delving with me into his wonderful stories can also be helped to reach toward a sense of their own multiple potentials and validate their search for completeness.

The ancient figure of the Dagda can help us recognize and bring into play potentials that were largely abandoned as we came to overvalue differentiation and idealize the one-sided rational ego that is often disconnected from other living systems and our own primordial vitality. Although we cannot and would not want to lose such hard-won capacities, the Dagda's image may facilitate a return to consciousness of a deeper sense of what it means to be human. Thus he stands as a kind of historical and cultural analogy to the symbols that, according to Jung, "frequently occur at the beginning of the individuation process [as manifestations of] . . . the *a priori* existence of potential wholeness."[8]

Often we lose access to these powerful symbols as we work through the plethora of issues on which our complexes require us to focus, but they remain in the background of consciousness. Then at certain later stages in life, we may be able to reconnect with the forms and processes of the archetype of wholeness, which, on an individual level, we can call the Self. This reconnection forms the basis for a new, balanced ego—one that can relate to the Self and to others with multileveled, permeable, expanded consciousness.

As evidenced in much contemporary science and philosophy, we have begun to reach toward this stage in some parts of the collective. Today with a differentiated and enlarged knowledge base regarding the consensual and physical world, explorers in many realms of discourse are moving toward an integrated understanding of events. Some psychologists, philosophers, mathematicians, biologists and physicists are reaching for and grounding intuitions of

---

[8] "The Psychology of the Child Archetype," *The Archetypes and the Collective Unconscious,* CW 9i, par. 278. (CW refers throughout to *The Collected Works of C.G. Jung)*

the interdependent processes underlying whole systems—reconnecting to what we might call a *gnosis* of the cosmic Self.

By looking at archetypal form patterns, systems, formal and final causes, and at chaos, information, field, and even multidimensional and "string" theories, students in many disciplines are reaching for perspectives that are, however, not entirely new. The holism we can again begin to celebrate was an aspect of early cultures. It was repressed in the West, relegated to so-called primitive peoples and primal layers of psyche. Now contemporary thinkers are rediscovering this perspective, enriched by the tools of science and mathematics and an extraordinary amount of new data about the physical universe.

Linking to what existed in these primal cultures before their wisdom was repressed not only restores strength and balance but also creates the possibility of recognizing and bringing into play developmental lines we have forgotten. In the healing arts, we are finally able to appreciate how much ancient and traditional methods can enrich our present scientific repertoire. On a personal level, too, we need to reclaim the potentials for wholeness that we have put aside to conform to the requirements of the groups in which we are socialized. Sometimes we can personally postpone taking these potentials out of their uneasy storage and dealing with them until a midlife crisis, but the current global turbulence affects so many of us that we no longer have the luxury to procrastinate.

This perspective on the initial conditions of wholeness helps me understand my own long-standing fascination with mythic patterns that bridge to archaic and magic levels of consciousness—where we can glimpse the beginnings of culture and the individual psyche. Often I have been drawn to explore material from times that existed long before nature and spirit, body and intellect were so deeply split in our culture's consciousness. This material expresses itself through symbols and processes of dynamic wholeness that were celebrated before the beginning of the heroic age in Western society. For me they convey the initial conditions of our culture and the deep structures of psyche. Since similar dynamic patterns shape all organisms, when we acknowledge them in ourselves we can begin to restore our severed relationships with natural, living systems.

The integrated vision we seek requires that we validate kinds of consciousness that do not depend only on linear logic, the separation of opposites and differentiated thinking. To sense fit between experience and image, we need also to operate through empathy, sensing intimately with and into the information that reveals itself to modes of awareness that exist in our bodies, emotions and imagination. With all of these we can seek the forms that express similarities of deep structure. We need to process such information in terms of isomorphism and analogy in order to allow our minds to play with its potentials. It is like fitting together a puzzle; we only sense what the whole might be as our attention slowly discovers meaningful correlations. At the outset and sometimes for long periods, we will have to stay with the search, not knowing, only trusting that relevant patterns will eventually emerge.

Ancient Celtic Sources

Looking back behind the modern severance of spirit from nature, we can find an important source of Western culture in the myths, art, music, folklore and traditions of pre-Celtic Ireland. This material is as important for understanding ourselves as Egyptian, Greco-Roman and Judeo-Christian influences—and just as vital a font of holistic perspective as Native American and Oriental traditions.

Irish lore can be difficult for the modern rational mind to understand. This is not surprising: its symbolism and rites have not been so molded by ages of literary reworking. Around the eighth century A.D., when church scribes first started to write down the tales, pieces of different ones were often patched together and amended, so it sometimes takes careful unstitching to make out the patterns of the originals. On the other hand, into the twentieth century, the ancient oral tradition was still thriving in areas where native Gaelic speakers lived—from Western Ireland and Brittany to Nova Scotia. There the stories, customs and calendar rituals, which persisted alongside or hidden within the dominant culture, kept alive the past.

These sources provide a direct link to the nature-based perspective of the Stone and Early Bronze Ages.

I personally love working with ancient Irish material for its poetry, its celebration of "the aristocracy of the imagination,"[9] and the authenticity of its emotional vividness and complexity. It is also very useful clinically, because it illuminates the patterns of the permeable psyche that lives on the edge of what we tend to label an alternate reality. This includes what we now call mystical, magical or imaginal modes of consciousness. Since we inevitably find pockets or layers of such borderland material in ourselves when we work deeply in analysis, it is a relief to discover a respectful, non-pathologizing approach to them that, alongside of personal history, can help orient us toward potential meanings and future developmental paths.

In this stratum, we can rediscover that what was later split into spirit and matter still flows from one abundant source. This material resonates with the ancestral, shamanic and shapeshifting roots of ancient European culture. Here the realms we separate into the spiritual, psychological and physical were still intimately interdependent and expressions of a common, sacred reality. Such a unified matrix lies deep in the Western psyche, even in the most rational of us.[10] It vibrates sympathetically with mystical-magical traditions around the globe. It beckons us to explore ourselves in depth to integrate its perspective with our usual rationality. It is not surprising that in my search for an image that might assuage my sense of loss, I would be drawn into these deepest layers of psyche.

Masculine Wholeness

The Dagda, and others like him, was a principal deity in ancient times. His myths sing of a potential for wholeness as it was seen through masculine imagery before Western culture began to grapple

---

[9] Robert O'Driscoll, Intro., in O'Driscoll, ed., *The Celtic Consciousness*, p. xvi.
[10] It comes to us through the layers of psyche that Jean Gebser calls archaic, magical and mythological, and Ken Wilber has renamed uroboric, typhonic and membership stages.

with issues of the heroic, myth-sung individual. After the tenth century A.D., he fell into the shadows as later cultures valued more precise differentiation, patrifocal ideals and behaviors, and the more one-sided, dominating, heroic ego. Now at the beginning of a new millennium, as we are crashing our way into the Aquarian Age, we require a new holistic model.

Today, for the most part, instead of images of masculine wholeness we have an array of prototypes. The pantheons of Greek and Roman gods display all their differences. This differentiation has expressed and supported rational Western consciousness. We can explore the evolution of each of these archetypal patterns and their changing contents through history. There are many images of the masculine in different cultures and ages—various portraits of son, trickster, hero, lover, father, king, wise old man, etc. What I needed was a single figure that could carry all of these aspects together, and such a one is hard to find. I thought of Jung's words: "We need some new foundations. [Therefore] we must dig down to the primitive [for] . . . a new experience of God."[11]

So I found myself digging, drawn to what the scholar Marie-Louise Sjoestedt calls "a mythico-ritual complex which belongs to the most ancient deposit that Irish tradition has preserved."[12] There, waiting for rediscovery, stood the Dagda.

My exploration revealed a male figure representing the Great Round in its vastness and interconnected processes. As warrior and king, Supreme Father and Lord of Great Knowledge and Druidry, this early horned god represents the balance to and respectful partner of three Great Goddesses. His stories reveal a wide range of attributes and functions. Not surprisingly, images reminiscent of the Dagda appear in modern clinical material when there is a need to expand one's sense of masculinity to encompass some of the earthy and cosmic proportions it held in ancient Irish culture. Thus, this material may inspire fuller development in both men and women,

---

[11] C.G. Jung, *Letters*, vol. 1, p. 40.
[12] *Gods and Heroes of the Celts*, p. 57.

who can then undertake the task of orienting toward and building a more holistic paradigm for each of us as individuals and for the culture of our endangered globe.

[Many men today are seeking new images of manliness that are relevant to all stages of life. They are willing to question the models given by their personal and collective fathers in order to discover better ways to relate to the feminine and to the unconscious, ways that do not sell out their intrinsic maleness and do not leave them tough, righteous, addicted, tormented, rueful or rootless.[13] Nor will many men now settle for the role of passive antihero, the overly soft, immature boy-man who hesitates to assert himself, remains a fearful, uncommitted, narcissistic dreamer or instead capitulates to women, ideals and gurus.] As a recent article states:

> The contemporary [Western] male character, as portrayed in fiction has no firm identity, no firm occupation, and little to tell except a story of decline. This portrait leaves men—and the women who haven't given up on them—at an impasse that calls on men to examine their collective story.[14]

Male and female authors have addressed these issues.[15] Almost every man I know well is struggling with them.

And women are too. As we rediscover and express a far greater range of energies than those that have been accorded us in most traditions, women have also been asking important questions: Where are the men who can meet us, not as seductive son-lovers who crave our mothering and the use of our bodies, nor as self-dramatizing sugar daddies who insist we remain passive daughters or become their trophy women? Where are the men who are not posturing, macho heroes who require our victimization and/or our applause for their aggression and sacrifices? Where are the men

---

[13] In contrast the sturdy, gentle firemen and police in New York cried openly, and they have been endlessly tender with the all the grieving folk drifting into their station houses bringing flowers, gratitude and tears.

[14] Tom Jenks, "Where are the men?" p. 14.

[15] See, for example, the works of Robert Bly, Robert Lawlor, Linda Leonard, John Rowan and Marion Woodman.

who are not trying to be senex authorities who devalue us to shore up their self-aggrandizing ideals? Where are the responsible, relatively secure, competent-enough, related partners willing to struggle honestly with themselves and us and the problems of contemporary life?

Increasingly, women, too, recognize the need to access new patterns of energy in themselves that they can respect and that support their self-respect. Given the slow return to contemporary culture of the goddess—the matrix underlying dynamic, interconnected fullness and expanded consciousness—both men and women need images of a masculine partner who can relate to her confidently as an equal.

Origins and Repression

The divine bull, one ancient form of the Dagda, represents an image of enormous procreative vitality and fearsome strength, as anyone who has worked with such animals on dairy farm or ranch knows.

My first encounters with a bull took place in my uncle's barn as I stood at a respectful distance from the huge breeding sire that served his cows. I was awed by the barely contained energy and by what I could now describe as an impression of sublime arrogance in the massive Holstein. His enormous, indifferent eyes and sheer presence reduced me to human insignificance and also excited fascination. Told to stand back from the bars around his stall, I had no doubt he could bend them if he chose. I wondered at the iron nose ring. Would it really enable only two men to lead him? That summer of latency, I hardly knew about sexual prowess, but I intuited something of the bull's colossal virility expanding through the bars.[16]

---

[16] I also helped the farmhands retrieve younger bulls when they broke through the fences. We would send a few dry cows after the strays so we could herd them all back and mend the wire. Always intimidated by their potential for violence, I was hardly reassured by the saying that "bulls were gentled by cows." Yet, it seemed to work. Now I wonder if that adage and the pastoral knowledge behind it was what motivated the chiefs of Bronze Age Ireland to send women to calm their own still-

Jung tells us that the bull is one of several theriomorphic sym-bols of the Self.[17] Not surprisingly, its form has been deified in early cultures around the world. Marija Gimbutas writes of the an-cient (pre-seventh millennium B.C.) bull and phallus god of old Europe.[18] The skulls of huge bulls grace the ancient shrine at Catal Huyuk in Anatolia. India has several bull gods. The Vedic, bel-lowing bull god Rudra lets forth his sperm to fertilize the world. Indra's bull represents "the fecundating power of heat and is related to the complex symbolism of fertility—horn, sky, water, lightning, [and] rain."[19] Shiva's bull, its hump like a snowy mountain, repre-sents sexual energy that the god can transform through his yogic practices. In ancient Sumer, Enlil, a majestic bull identified with the constellation of Taurus, sits enthroned as lord of the heavens. The Chaldean moon god Ur is called "the mighty young bull of the sky."[20]

Egyptian Osiris, god of the underworld and the moon, has a bull form. In Palestine, the bull god El symbolizes the powers of crea-tion. While Moses proscribed worship of the golden calf, the first letter of the Hebrew alphabet is *aleph,* which means bull, and sym-bolizes the moon in its first week. The bull god in China is a spirit of the wind and rain. In Greek myth the bull is connected with Po-seidon, the bull of the sea, with ecstatic Dionysus, and with Zeus, who assumed bull form to carry off Europa. The Minotaur of the Cretan labyrinth, the offspring of Poseidon and a human queen, is a monstrous amalgam of bull and man. Later, in the second century A.D., devotees of a cult of Cybele gained the force of the bull and its immortal spirit through the sacrificial rites of the *taurobolium*—an initiation through baptism in bull blood. In the worship of the

---

raging warriors. In two incidents women with bared breasts go forth to meet Cuchullain when he returns to court still possessed by his invincible war frenzy. See Perera, "Ritual Integration of Aggression in Psychotherapy," pp. 246ff.

[17] *Aion,* CW 9ii, par. 356.

[18] *The Goddesses and Gods of Old Europe: Myths and Cult Images,* pp. 216ff.

[19] Jean Chevalier et al., *The Penguin Dictionary of Symbols,* p. 131.

[20] Ibid, p. 132.

Persian god Mithras, spread by the legions throughout Roman Europe, sacrifice of the bull symbolized the god's conquest of the powers of evil and the regeneration of the world through the release of the animal's blood, marrow and seed.

In ancient Ireland, too, the early inhabitants, whose wealth was often measured in the number of their cows, worshipped various horned animals, among them the bull. It was originally associated with the fertilizing sun, with knowledge of plowing and herds, with grain, the harvest feast, and capacities to influence time and the weather. As in other cultures, the sacred bull in Ireland conveys much of the agrarian and pastoral legacy of the Neolithic Age. There is evidence from the third millennium B.C. to suggest bull rituals at various harvest festivals.[21] Folk legends of the origin of Lughnasa at three major sites tell of a bull that belongs to the pagan deity of the hilltop. Sacrificed during the assembly, perhaps at a sacred enclosure near the foot of the mountain, the bull was ritually reborn either when his skin was stuffed and the effigy was paraded before the assembly, or when a young bull was substituted to take the slain bull god's place.[22]

At the huge Crom Dubh Henge near Loch Gur in Munster, bull feasts are also associated with Samain, the hallowed assembly celebrated around November 1st to mark the culling of the herds. The tallest megalith in this circle is known traditionally as the *Crom Dubh*. The sun sets at summer's end behind two horn stones about three-fifths of the circumference away from that megalith. Layers of organic debris left behind these horns suggest that the bull was roasted and devoured during ritual feasts.[23] The stone circle itself was erected ca. 2500 B.C. with alignments to the sunsets and sunrises that occur on the four Neolithic agricultural feasts. These holy days were celebrated by the tribes gathering at *Beltane*, May 1st, to

---

[21] Michael Dames, *Mythic Ireland*, pp. 103ff.

[22] Maire MacNeill, *The Festival of Lughnasa: A Study of the Survival of the Celtic Festival of the Beginning of Harvest*, pp. 410ff., 422.

[23] Dames, *Mythic Ireland*, pp. 104ff.

mark the beginning of the summer year; at *Lughnasa,* now called Garland Sunday, the feast of first fruits; at *Samain,* November 1st, the feast marking the death of the summer year; and at *Imbolc,* the February 1st feast day of the triple goddess Brigid, when there were rituals of first plowing and the spring birthing in the herds. Thus the pre-Celtic folk honored the bull god and his partner throughout the cycle of the year.

In Ireland, a human form of this ancient animal god was titled *Crom.* Identical with the food-providing Dagda, this figure "brings the light, the darkness, and the change of seasons."[24] The word *Crom* means bent or crooked, suggesting that his back was bowed over as he carried the first sheaf of grain from the fields. This was the sheaf representing the corn maiden *Eithne* (kernel or grain).

The Bronze Age tribes continued the veneration, often metamorphosing the bull into other divine animals to represent primal energy in its various shapes. In one tale, two divine pig-keepers shapeshift into birds of prey, undersea creatures, stags, warriors, phantoms, dragons and life-engendering maggots before they become bulls. The series may have significance for the transformations required of a shaman, but it also underlines the pre-Celtic inclusivity and fluidity of form through which human and nonhuman link in a cosmic continuum.[25] At other times the supernatural bull or ox was anthropomorphized.[26]

The Celtic warrior aristocracies associated the powers of the primeval and fertile bull god with fierceness in battle—just as Mediterranean cultures turned Mars, the old fertility deity, into their god of war. In an Irish text deriving from the oral tradition of the late Bronze Age, we can sense the sheer animal magnitude of the Celtic bull god:

---

[24] Patrick K. Ford, "Aspects of the Patrician Legend," in Patrick K. Ford, ed., *Celtic Folklore and Christianity,* p. 35.

[25] Thomas Kinsella, ed. and trans., *The Tain (Tain Bo Cuailnge),* pp. 48f.

[26] Anne Ross, *Pagan Celtic Britain: Studies in Iconography and Tradition,* pp. 302ff.

dark brown dire haughty with young health
horrific overwhelming ferocious
full of craft
furious fiery flanks narrow
brave brutal thick breasted
curly browed head cocked high
growling and eyes glaring
tough maned neck thick and strong
snorting mightly in muzzle and eye
with a true bull's brow
and a wave's charge
and a royal wrath
and the rush of a bear
and a beast's rage
and a bandit's stab
and a lion's fury.
Thirty grown boys could take
their place from rump to nape
—a hero to his herd at morning
foolhardy at the herd's head
to his cows the beloved
to husbandmen a [support] . . .
the father of great beasts
[he] overlooks the ox[en] of the earth.[27]

This divine bull is both a fierce, warlike beast, the fertile father of his flock, and the sustainer of human agriculture. As we shall see, the stories of the Dagda include these elements and amplify them to reveal a figure of magnificent wholeness.

However, when we look at the mighty horned god later in Ireland, we can see his form and energies have undergone the workings of cultural repression. The natural and mythic coherence of the Dagda's figure was forgotten, and the qualities that remain were distorted to fit new ideals. Thus, the authorities of succeeding epochs co-opted, diminished or demonized the revered powers and symbols of the ancient bull god. The process is analogous to what happens to us individually as we are socialized and lose free access

[27] Kinsella, *The Tain,* pp. 49f.

to the embodied energies and fluid structures of consciousness that are prominent in early childhood. When the repression is too severe, our psychological vitality may suffer the same fate as the bull god, becoming distorted or forced underground.

Such radical cultural repression began in Ireland after the coming of St. Patrick's mission in the fifth century A.D. It was exacerbated by the Roman and later Norman feudal church use of the Patrician legends to authorize their dogma. But the old stories themselves also reveal ambivalence, since reverence for the powers of the earthy god remained strong among the agricultural and herding folk. The struggle between pagan and Christian perspectives plays out in the tales. Thus the giant bull was said to be a mighty servant of the druids who opposed Patrick. In one account the druids "raised a bull that [nightly] gored the walls of the wee church to bits" to prevent St. Patrick from claiming the "gentle place" on Carrickatuke where Lughnasa assemblies and feasting were held from times immemorial. "And in the end Patrick lost heart and went [away to build his church in] Armagh."[28] Eventually, and with noteworthy ambivalence, this protective, old pagan "bull was routed, killed and buried, but the marks of its leaps are still shown, as is the stone over its grave, which stone is believed to confer virility."[29]

Many similar folk tales of fierce and untamable bulls or bulls guarding ancient treasure who are overcome by a saint were gathered into the twentieth century in Ireland.[30] They suggest psychologically that the powers of our animal nature resist socialization and continue to guard treasured aspects of life, aspects that are problematic in cultures that seek to repress instinctual energy.

Early medieval accounts redefine the old god Crom in his circle of stones as "the King Idol of Erin." They call him a bloodthirsty "Moloch . . . [a mere] withered hump of mists, hulking over every

---

[28] MacNeill, *Festival of Lughnasa*, p. 158.

[29] Ibid., p. 396.

[30] Ibid., pp. 393ff., 436ff., 474ff.

path, refusing the eternal kingdom," although his great megalith is still defined as "the pivot figure . . . of gold."[31] And those telling the old place-name legends still imply that Crom's circle of stones is an ancient holy site. It lies on what they still call "The Plain of Adoration."[32] Nonetheless, the stones and the megalith are now negativized and made cruel, no longer to be adored. Crom is damned as an enslaving idol, akin to the Biblical Golden Calf.

> Before the coming of Patrick [the scribe's tale goes], Crom, the Stooped One, was the god of every people that occupied Ireland. It is to him they used to offer the first-born of every stock and the first-born of every family. The king of Ireland . . . came at Samuin, together with the men and women of Ireland, to adore him.[33]

But the adoration was deplored. They had to bow down so their noses and knees broke. The people were said to give terrible sacrifices in return for the bull god's gifts of milk, grain and herds. The scribes tell us that "For him ingloriously they slew their hapless first-borns with much wailing and peril, to pour their blood around Crom."[34] St. Patrick, like Moses, is to be revered as the redeemer from such barbarity. Thus, with a miracle, he makes the once powerful and adored megalith bow down to him, or, in another story, he overturns it and causes the other stones in the circle to sink into the ground.

In other tales of St. Patrick, a man named Crom is said to be one of his main adversaries—as big a problem for the new religion as the snakes, which never existed in Ireland but were associated with horned divinities.[35] This Crom is now the pagan owner of a miraculous and immortal bull. In one story Patrick claims the animal to feed his followers, and then he asserts his Christian god's power

---

[31] John Montague, "The Plain of Adoration, from the Irish, Eleventh Century," in *John Montague: Collected Poems*, pp. 273f.

[32] Ninth century A.D. See Ford, "Aspects of the Patrician Legend," p. 46.

[33] Alwyn Rees and Brinley Rees, *Celtic Heritage: Ancient Tradition in Ireland and Wales*, p. 196.

[34] Ford, "Aspects of the Patrician Legend," p. 46.

[35] Ibid., pp. 34f, 43ff.

to restore it to life. In another tale, the saint maddens the bull and has its herdsman owner tossed "so high that when he came to the ground he was dead."[36] Proclaiming the dominance of the god of a new religion, Patrick's stories manifest the process of transforming the ancient horned god into a demon that can be vanquished. Thus in Ireland, the Church identified the bull, as well as the serpent, with Satan.

A recently collected folk legend recounts another version of the suppression of the bull god.[37] Once in old England near the village of Hissington, there was a great bull that terrorized the countryside. By some not-divulged feat, a Christian priest captured the mighty creature and managed to confine it inside the local church. He gained control over the beast by reciting prayers and reading the Bible. As he did so, the bull magically shrank to the size of a terrier, a little Jack Russell. By then it was night. The candle went out, the reading stopped. The priest, thinking his work done, fell asleep. Of course, the bull started to grow again. By morning it was so large it was cracking the walls of the church. The anxious padre had to begin all over again. This time he trapped the tiny animal in a boot and, like St. Patrick in Ireland, he buried it—this time under the threshold of the church, to be tromped upon by every parishioner. However, the story warns, if that little bull is ever dug up, it will grow to its original size. So beware the return of the repressed!

I love this wonderful tale of the vigorous Celtic bull god still roaming among the folk. He is considered to be too earthy and sexually potent, hence too dangerous and terrorizing in the landscape of a "good" parish. Certainly his energies are too disturbing for the well-being of a man of the cloth, perhaps overly troubled by the animal passions that spoil his ambition to live up to his spiritual ideals. The priest diminishes the power of the ancient horned one by invoking scripture. He could certainly find Biblical references to bullocks as sin offerings as well the prophet Isaiah's warning not to

---

36 Ibid., pp. 43ff.

37 Ralph Whitlock, *In Search of Lost Gods: A Guide to British Folklore*, p. 16.

delight in the blood of bulls. He might have read Amos's curse on the women who still worshipped the goddess—"Woe unto you, ye cows of Bashan" (Amos 4:1), and Moses' smashing of the Golden Calf (Exod. 32:20). Overturning the old god's powers with the magic words of his holy book, the priest finally secures what is left of animal nature under the threshold. In many Celtic stories the threshold figures prominently because it is spatially between the worlds of the sacred and the secular. And here it is held in a boot—imprisoned in the Christian protection of the human standpoint that keeps our feet from being in direct contact with nature, earth and our own potential fullness. The firm leather crust of the boot helps us trample the urges that might threaten ideals of chastity and obedience to such doctrine.

In the dogma of the Church, the bull of Hissington—like Pan, Dionysus and the Dagda—becomes the horned and cloven-hoofed devil. Alternatively the Church co-opts and tames his powers, and he is transformed into a saint, like the Breton St. Edern, whose familiars are the horned animals he now protects and blesses. In Brittany the bull god also lives on as St. Cornely, named for his horns but now patron of the herds, depicted in art with his gentle familiar, a bull.

On a folk level, reverence persists for the horned lord of the Old Religion and the circle of life and death. Thus we find Robin Goodfellow is the stag-horned Green Man, who dances with the witches and lives on in tales of Robin Hood. Carved faces of the smiling Green Man peer out from the corners of British churches. The folk rituals of old Crom, the Dagda, and other horned gods endure throughout the British Isles. Into the nineteenth century at *Samain*—our Halloween—just as they did in ancient times at the stone circle near Loch Gur, every household around Galway Bay skinned and roasted a bull in honor of the solar god sinking into the underworld of winter. Even the bull god's name lives on in the Christian calendar as *Cromm Duibv Domnaigh,* Black Stoop Sunday. Thus the first Sunday of August, the Neolithic harvest festival and ritual offering of the first fruits to the old god, still carries his name. We sense reverberations of old Crom, the bountiful one, still bending under the weight of the sacred first sheaf he carries yearly from the fields.[38]

At Mount Callan on Lughnasa the custom of strewing flowers to honor him also persists in Ireland. Even now, in Berkshire, England, villagers hold parades with a man chosen from the Morris dancers to be "The Mock Mayor of Ox Street."[39] He wears the old horned crown of the pagan bull. And in Nottinghamshire, an old wellspring continues to be known as "Bull Well."[40]

Not only is there a revival of interest in such folk material today, there are several contemporary music groups and songs called "Dagda."[41] And on Broadway there is a powerful play by Edward Albee called after another horned divinity, "The Goat." It portrays a modern architect in midlife just awarded a coveted commission to design a megalopolis on the Great Plains of the United States. We sense his ambivalence and recognize that the grand urban scheme will also bring vast changes to the natural world. While roaming farmland nearer to his perfectly appointed city apartment, with its sterilized versions of primitive art, the architect has fallen in love with a white goat. Drawn to her innocent eyes and warm, pungent body, he becomes her lover. His poignant compulsion for (re)union with the horned goddess of nature disorients him and arouses anxious laughter in the audience. In the play it also evokes horror in his uncomprehending television producer friend, and contempt and rage in his urban wife. The success-driven producer attacks him as madly endangering his career. His sophisticated wife calls him bestial, even more disgusting, she says, than the father and brothers who together enjoyed their repeated incest of the girl child in the family: "At least they are human."

Torn between his love for wife and horned animal, the protago-

---

[38] Dames, *Mythic Ireland,* p. 101.
[39] Whitlock, *In Search of Lost Gods,* p. 144.
[40] Personal communication, Ann Morley.
[41] Personal communication, Susan Shaughnessy.

nist cannot find his own voice or understand himself. Vengefully, his wife murders the goat. The drama suggests analogies to Christ and the pure, Biblical scapegoat. But the animal in the play is female, like an old Celtic horned goddess of nature,[42] like pre-Celtic Boann, the cow goddess who was one partner of the Dagda.

---

[42] See Ross, *Pagan Celtic Britain,* pp. 144, 217, plate 45c and fig. 103.

3

The Dagda

Early Celtic material offers a rich store of male figures who part-
nered the earth goddess and did not separate from nor dominate
nature and the revered feminine as radically as the male figures we
see in the myths of Mediterranean cultures. We would never find a
goddess-killing Marduk or St. George in Ireland even after Ro-
manized Christianity arrived at its feudal, Norman phase. Into medieval times, the person of the Celtic queen still represented the deity of the land. Romanesque sculptures of the goddess as Sheela-na-
gig, with her legs outspread to display her fruitful vulva, sat on the
walls of cemeteries, feudal churches and castles to assert that even
the Norman church and lords were guarded and supported by the
Great Goddess of the lands and people they sought to dominate.[43]

In general, Celtic deities are more aboriginal than classical ones,
even though Roman writers created pantheons for them, and Christian scribes in Ireland made neat genealogies to link up groups of
Celtic gods. The functions of the ancient figures were not as differentiated as those of later deities were. Each had a wide range of
powers and manifestations. Thus, most of the early Celtic gods
could heal, nourish, protect and destroy. They were civilizing inno-
vators, battle leaders and ancestor kings who modeled the wisdom
and skills necessary for cultural survival. They were also magi-
cians, in a culture that did not separate the sacred and the magical.
And they all had intimate connections to the animal realm, sometimes shape shifting from one to another manifestation of the archetypal energies they represented. Usually there was one all-
purpose divinity of each tribe. This figure represented the Self in
masculine terms. He was the partner of the Great Goddess who
symbolized life's processes and the earth on which the tribe lived.

---

[43] See Perera, *Celtic Queen Maeve*, pp. 56ff.

We can find out more about the primordial bull god in various legends and in a story that stands at the center of Irish mythology.[44] *The Second Battle of Maige Tuired* is a tale of pseudo history describing the contest between some deities of pagan Ireland, the *Tuatha de Danaan* (People of the Goddess Dana or Ana), and their enemies. The texts were written down in the ninth century but were based in the much earlier tradition that was passed by storytellers from mouth to ear. It is through this oral transmission from "the most ancient deposit that Irish tradition has preserved,"[45] that we receive much Dagda material. We can peer through its dark glass to find the cluster of qualities originally attributed to the ancient, all-purpose, protean bull god.

The name *In Dagda* translates as "The Good God." It derives from *Dago Devos*, the old Irish version of Good, *Deiwos* or *Dyeus*, the name of a Bronze Age, Indo-European sky god. As we have seen, however, his figure is far more ancient. He is even associated with the pre-Celtic stratum of sun-lore and fertility evident in the architecture of the fourth millennium temple at Newgrange, which, according to a tradition we will examine later, was built by the Dagda.[46] We have no known visual representations of him specifically in Ireland, except for the modern sculpture by Michael Quirke that graces the cover of this book.[47] Nonetheless, there are similar

---

[44] The oldest extant version, written in the first half of the sixteenth century on a vellum manuscript now in the British Museum, was based on an Old and Middle Irish text of the ninth century copied in the eleventh or twelfth. See Elizabeth A. Gray, ed., *Cath Maige Tuired: The Second Battle of Mag Tuired,* pp. 1, 11.

[45] Sjoestedt, *Gods and Heroes,* p. 57.

[46] Daithi O hOgian, *The Sacred Isle: Belief and Religion in Pre-Christian Ireland,* p. 60.

[47] Paul Gauguin carved a handsome self-portrait of himself as a savage with bull horns, and drew the figure peering lustily at a nude woman. (See "Head with Horns: Polynesian Beauty with Evil Spirit," in Colta Ives and Susan Stein, *The Lure of the Exotic: Gauguin in New York Collections,* pp. 134ff.) Identified by curators as suggesting his own devilish nature, the form harks back to the Breton Saint Edern, patron of horned animals, and the older horned-god Celtic traditions still flourishing in Gauguin's day in Brittany. Picasso's fascination with the Minotaur of Crete is another example of the bull god's modern renaissance.

figures from many Celtic areas.

The storytellers name the Dagda "Lord of Great Knowledge" or "All-Knowing Noble," master of all arts and knowledge, the god of Magic and time. Both Bull and Horseman, he was also called "Supreme Father of All."[48] In Sligo today, some folk refer to him affectionately as *Dagda Mor* or "Big Daddy." And big he is— massive and momentous. He "marched through all of Erin: broader was his face than half a plain."[49]

In one ninth-century A.D. manuscript, he is described as "a very big and tall man with remarkable eyes, thighs, and shoulders, and a fine gray cloak about him."[50] Using prodigious strength, he clears twelve plains in one night and digs twelve rivers in another. Single-handedly, he builds massive forts and ramparts and tosses about huge glacial boulders in his spare time. One craggy boulder near Lugh's Seat in County Sligo is said, even today, to look like him.

Although some medieval writers gave him a genealogy and told tales of his death,[51] earlier ones affirm him as the original and still living progenitor of his people and the principle of fertility itself. He has thus been equated with the Gallic figure whom the Romans called "Dis Pater," a divine ancestor, after their Pluto. He was nick-named *Aedh Alainn*, "Beautiful Fire," and *Ruadh Ro-fhessa*, "Ruddy One of Great Wisdom,"[52] implying the ruddy of sun rise and set, not the noon sun. The sun was feminine in much early Irish lore, and the Dagda is connected with its crossings to and from

---

[48] This pairing of horse and bull is similar to that in the Paleolithic caves of France. See André Leroi-Gourhan, *Treasures of Prehistoric Art*. The Dagda is also identified as Cera, Aed Abaid of Ess Ruad, Dagan, and Cratan Cain. See Gray, *Cath Maige Tuired*, p. 121.

[49] Edward Gwynn, ed., *The Metrical Dindschenchas*, vol. 4, p. 105.

[50] O hOgian, *The Sacred Isle*, p. 62.

[51] Pseudo historians say that he met his death as the result of a wound inflicted by the Ceithleann, wife of Balar, with whom he engaged in single combat in the Second Battle of Mag Tuired. She stabbed him with a javelin, creating a wound that troubled him for the eighty years he ruled the Tuatha after Lugh. See Daithi O hOgian, *Myth, Legend and Romance*, p. 146.

[52] O hOgian, *The Sacred Isle*, p. 60.

night, with thresholds and liminality, all of which today we would consider unusual for the all-powerful masculine.

One of the Dagda's sexual partners asks him to tell her his name. He teasingly gives her one of them, then another. Like all deities, he is too encompassing to be held in words, but she banters and gains the spectrum of him. Then this goddess uses the names as an incantation to make him do what she wants—to carry her on his back and make love. He cooperates with the goddess as he always does. And after being assured of his friendship, potency and equal strength, she, in turn, offers her help to his tribe.

This primordial, agricultural goddess ritually invokes his grandeur and fullness in Neolithic and Bronze Age terms:

Horned man [she says],[53] Big bellied One, Ample One, Hacking One, Excrement, Warrior, Beautiful One, Talkative One, Proud One, Power, Authority, Source, Great Father, Existence [or Being], Regeneration of the World, War Chariot, Triad, Wheel, King, Reckoner, Rejecter/Refuser, Great Decline or Ebb.[54]

While the translation of some terms in the still longer list is unsure, the names circumambulate a vastness that includes abundance and war as well as civilizing, ruling and transcendent capacities. They form a gigantic, breathtaking conglomeration of attributes. The images flow and wind to evoke many capacities and a nearly cosmic wholeness—all bound together as in a Celtic, coiling, interlace design. And the Dagda is the only god in early Celtic literature actually to be named Horned Man *(Fer Benn)*, although there is one sculpture from Gaul identified by the Latinized word, *Cernunnos,* the Horned One, and there are many stone and bronze repre-

---

[53] In *Cath Maige Tuired* Gray translates *Fer Benn* as peaked man, although the word *benn* also means horned when applied to mountains and animals (see Oxford Irish Dictionary). The Dagda, partner of the cow goddess Boan and caller of the Fomorian cows must be a bull god, just as Fergus, partner of Flidias, a deer goddess, must have been a stag god. Nonetheless I had no confirmation that Dagda was named as horned until I found the Irish text and checked the old Irish dictionary.

[54] Tentative translations by Gray, *Cath Maige Tuired,* pp. 48f., and others.

sentations of human deities with horns.[55]

In his stories we will see the Dagda as the embodiment of earthy vitality and procreative power, a mighty warrior, a generous and just ruler, a lover and mate of the Great Goddesses, a herdsman of cattle, the original master of druidry. He is a healer, an architect and builder, a musician and a wise, generous chieftain-father to his children and people. We can view him as a combination of fierce and fertile Mars, passionate ruling Zeus, powerful Thor, androgynous Dionysus and Hermes, wise Odin, and dark transformative Pluto. He has been called "a primal father deity of enormous power"[56] and fullness, much like the supreme, wondrous, generous, benevolent, strong and wise guardian-father of a young child. It is a rich wholeness befitting the paternal ruler of the tribe and of the tribe of gods. And yet sometimes he is also foolish and incompetent, needing his own son to bail him out. Invariably he models generosity and respect for those who come after him or have different perspectives.

When given a genealogy in medieval times, he was said to be half Fomorian. Thus through his father, he represents the group of ancient magician gods associated with fecundity, the sea and the Early Stone Age agricultural inhabitants of Ireland. These were his people's enemies in the Second Battle of Mag Tuired, pushed away, yet still living on the outskirts and in the sea. His mother, the great triple goddess Brigid, who is also sometimes called his three daughters by scribes who didn't approve of the Old Religion, is said to be from the Tuatha, the people of the Goddess Danaan.

These gods reached Ireland later than the Fomorians, coming in mists from the same mysterious northern islands.[57] With this double ancestry, the Dagda bridges the culture of megalithic peoples to those of the Celtic Bronze Age. Like many Celtic deities and the

---

[55] See Ross, *Pagan Celtic Britain*, pp. 333ff. There are several men described as horned in Conchobar's army because of the silver or copper horns (or helmets) they wore. See Kinsella, ed., *The Tain*, pp. 219ff.

[56] Marie-Louise Sjoestedt, *Gods and Heroes of the Celts*, p. 125.

[57] Called Lochlainn, see Gray, *Cath Maige Tuired*, pp. 90f.

gods of India, the Dagda probably appeared in triune form to show intensification in visual terms, like early three-faced Vedic deities.

Omniscient and omnipotent, he is good at everything. This goodness is neither moral nor perfectionistic. Among the ancient Celts there is no superego as we know it. Their code of behavior is based on honor and shame before collective consciousness, not individual guilt. Like forces of nature and the gods of Greece, the old Irish deities are amoral. The Dagda kills, consorts with enemies, uses trickery, suffers role reversals and foolishness as part of Being. And all shamelessly. He is no more monogamous than the goddesses he loves. He is not morally good in terms of any righteous ideal we might support. But he is honorable and complete, holding opposing energies in balance. He has functional, not normative, goodness. He is good at everything, at whatever the situation requires. When his turn came at the council before battle to say what he would accomplish for his tribe, he said he would do all that the other gods had promised. He would shake the mountains, control the waters, rain fire on their enemies, and bind up their courage and skill while increasing the might of his own warriors and fighting fiercely using his great club.

"You are the Dagda ['the Good God']!" said everyone; and "Dagda" stuck to him from that time on.[58]

The Dagda's title points to magical and practical omnipotence. Representing aggression, fertility and leadership, he is supremely competent in these areas that underlie all Indo-European cultures.[59] As we shall see, each one of these aspects can be connected with his partnership with a Great Goddess—the first with the Morrigan, a triple goddess of life, death and war; the second with the unnamed princess of the earthy Fomorian gods (the one who calls him all of his names); and the third with Boann, the white cow goddess of Newgrange, the River Boyne, and the earth and starry sky.

---

[58] Ibid., p. 45.
[59] See George Dumezil, *Gods of the Ancient Northmen.*

4

Partial Integration Through Opposition

The God as Warrior

As the fierce, bull god protector of his tribe and its land and herds, the Dagda uses brute strength as well as magical power to battle his enemies and shore up his own forces. There is suggestive evidence of an ancient ritual contest of rival bulls in a megalithic stone circle dated around 2500 B.C. With the coming of the Bronze Age in Ireland, such battles were carried on between humans after ritual assemblies. Then the clansmen and boys of rival chiefs engaged in faction fights and fierce games of hurley—a game perhaps arising from the use of sticks made from the shin bones of the bull.[60]

In human form, the mighty and "swift Dagda was deadly as a poison draught."[61] Several of his names refer to his warrior role: "Horned Man," "Hacking One," "Warrior," "Proud One," "Power," and "War Chariot." In their first great conquest in Ireland, his people make him their war leader. With one end of his mighty club he kills nine warriors with a single blow, and with the other end he revives nine. He uses the club to expel a sea monster and make the sea recede to uncover the great plain of Mag Muirthemne.[62] Unlike the actions of later heroes, his do not involve slaying this dragon aspect of the Great Goddess. He simply shoves her and her waters off land he wants to claim for settlement, limiting the powers of the chaotic abyss in order to promote civilization.

Throughout his mythology he uses aggression to make and hold boundaries against anything that would threaten the required order. He is a bringer of culture, separating it from the watery abyss, but

---

[60] Dames, *Mythic Ireland,* pp. 102ff., and Ford, ed., *Celtic Folklore,* p. 43.

[61] Gwynn, *Metrical Dindschenchas,* p. 93.

[62] Gray, *Cath Maige Tuired,* p. 121 (text of tenth century A.D.).

he also remains allied with the goddesses of earth, rivers and sky. And as we shall see later, this ongoing relationship with the feminine principle suggests a model of psychological development that is again becoming important in our time.

In all of these acts, the Dagda represents the aggressive capacity needed for active claiming and guardianship. His club is not a sophisticated weapon, like a sword that is used make sharp discriminations, but he wields it with deadly effect. It evokes images of Stone Age hacking, smashing brutality. Its form is closely allied to the war club of Ogma, Irish god of war and oral poetry, who is said to be one of his sons, and to the ax and mallet of the "Good Striker" Succelos, a Gallic woodsman and builder god. Thus it is both a weapon to be used against outside threats to tribal order and a tool to clear land in order to construct new buildings. Like many early tools, it combines functions, making it adaptable to life's varying needs.

In warrior mode, the Dagda represents an early form of the archetype underlying the ideal of Western masculine identity and the powers of focused mental discrimination that clearly separate observed from observer. Unlike later warriors who use spear and sword and laser-guided bombs, he both attacks his adversaries with one end of his club and holds the opposites together within its wholeness, for the other end can revive the dead. His capacity to embody balanced order is too often lost to warriors of subsequent ages.

The Bronze Age Warrior

Later in the mythology, the functions the Dagda holds together are distributed over several figures. With the loss of his fullness, a more specialized form of the warrior appeared. As Irish culture developed under the impact of the Bronze and Iron Age invasions of aristocratic Celtic tribes, we find a new ideal supplanting that of the multifunctional Dagda.

With excitingly portrayed, romanticized violence, youthful warriors serving their local chiefs individually and in brotherly bands crush, stab and split the original unity symbolized by the old god and the increasingly devalued goddess. The young warrior battles to conquer specific parts of her land. With jubilant aggression, he stands firmly for male dominance and against interdependency with the matrix. With flagrant exhibitionism, he courts death to prove his individual grandeur. This single-pointed, focused, adversarial warrior is the figure with which we are more familiar. And we know many stories extolling the type, whether the hero be named Marduk, who cuts up the earth goddess Tiamat, or Achilles or Cuchullain, invincible and prototypical battlers of Greece and Ireland respectively. In Christianity, we find them as models of youthful fervor in St. George, vanquisher of the mother dragon, and St. Joan, a mystic dressed in man's armor to fight against the enemies of her king.

The warrior requires an opponent. Without one there is no need to fight to survive or prove one's power. Within our psyches, such honed aggression precipitates conflict and ensures the control of one part over another. When we seek to destroy what is considered shameful or bad rather than accept, tame it and find its balance within our whole psyche, our inner life becomes a war. We will look later here at the relation of such heroic ego ideals to all that is repressed into the shadows while we try to stand strong, bright and righteous. Donna Germano puts it poignantly, "In civilizations that war, the human and vulnerable side of the warrior is rarely told."[63]

The modern Western world prizes aggressive consciousness. As we overvalue domination, we also overvalue the polarizing forms of rational consciousness. Moving away from holism and the original ground of matrix consciousness and matter, we perceived intellect separate from body, and matter itself cut up into a collection of smaller and smaller pieces to be verbally classified and worked

---

[63] *Women and the Tears of Men*, p. 12. Increasingly ignored as well is the old Irish proverb, "Never give a sword to a man who can't dance"—the title of a workshop led by Shaun Shaughnessy, 2002. Warrior culture converts the great circle dances of life and death that are part of hunting and agricultural ritual. They become war dances to rouse energy against a foe and expressions of individual prowess.

over. In identity with this intellectual style, our culture has often dismissed other forms of consciousness and even sought to destroy them by devaluing them.

Thus, for example, in line with the positivism arising from post-Enlightenment thought, Freud and some of his early followers weighted secondary process over primary. Even in some Jungian writing, the solar warrior who divides up the matrix, guards specific, partial territory, and separates from and cuts down the enemy other has been extolled as the bringer of consciousness. Increasingly however, psychologists and philosophers argue for examining the greater range and complexity of forms of consciousness that we do use. These forms are related to imaginal and undirected thinking and to perceptions arising from empathic resonance within interpersonal relationships and archetypal fields.

Jung, Donald Winnicott and Jean Gebser urged us to recognize that the kind of rational mentation that operates through contrasting opposites and taking issues apart is only one form of consciousness. It is important to enable us to become separate enough from the sensations and emotions to develop an observing and self-reflective stance. But we also need to reexamine the ways we are conscious through the body and through our creative, imaginal outpourings.

Just as it is important to have access to separative consciousness within the whole spectrum, so the warrior is indeed an important archetype for those who need to claim their aggressive drive and assert individual mastery. The qualities of the warrior are still valuable for those lacking conscious relationship to instinctual assertive energy. Instead of using it to guard themselves and support their mastery of a problem, such people tend to suffer aggression as an uncontrolled eruption or as self-destructiveness. Those men and women who have feared to relate to aggressive and competitive drives may need to work through aspects of the warrior myth as they claim their powers for self-assertion.[64]

---

[64] See Perera, "Ritual Integration of Aggression in Psychotherapy," pp. 233ff.

The Dagda and Cuchullain

In the Dagda mythology, the warrior aspect is only one part of the whole. In the Bronze Age, the warrior becomes a type unto itself. Young Cuchullain is extolled as the quintessential warrior of Ulster. Standing alone for the glory of his tribe against all the forces of the mighty Irish goddess Maeve, he represents the ideal of one-sided, ardent, phallic assertion and the desire to dominate. While we now see these qualities in some young children, we might, especially if they persisted into adulthood, call them aspects of a narcissistic character disorder. In the Bronze Age, they were not intimations of pathology, however, but essential aspects of the model of the new warrior caste.

Like the weapon in his hand and the fighting horns of the bull, the Bronze Age warrior represents idealized violence and the willingness to be possessed by such exciting power. In identity with aggression and filled with its ardor, young Cuchullain transforms into a single-focused berserker. When the rage is on him, he undergoes his much admired "warp spasm."[65] His whole body swells and twists, his features distort, a fierce hero's horn of light leaps high from his head. He becomes terrifying and invincible. This great guardian of Ulster destroys anything and anyone that would threaten his tribal land and ideals. He hones such instinctive fervor and focuses it so he can win with skill and pride. Cuchullain's deliciously exhibitionistic displays of spear, sword, shield, leaping, and chariot-driving feats—some of which he gained from his teacher, the warrior goddess Scathach—earns him the adoration of his contemporaries.

As a solar hero with a gigantic temper and heat enough to melt snow for twenty feet around him, he has a primary sense of responsibility to uphold his own pride and honor and that of the patrifocal chief and warriors with whom he is identified. Unless awakened suddenly from sleep, his aggression is disciplined and serves the

---

[65] Kinsella, ed., *The Tain*, pp. 150ff.

tribal king.[66] Such bravery, skill and furor gain him the hero's portion at royal feasts and the reputation of being Ireland's invincible, truly grand guardian. Honorable reputation is life to the warrior hero, and Cuchullain wins it at every turn. Of all the heroes of Ulster, only he fearlessly embodies the ideal and discipline of his caste; only he dares to accept the challenge to behead the old cosmic vegetation giant CuRoi and then honorably and courageously return to suffer the same blow. He is the early Irish model for Gawain in the medieval tale of the Green Knight.

In sharp contrast to the much broader and also care-giving, fatherly, regal and wise Dagda, Cuchullain is the warrior who knowingly kills his own talented young son in battle to honor himself and Ulster. He even enhances his own renown, because he has guaranteed that the boy is already his peer. The lad has defeated the best of the other warriors sent to greet him and ask his name, a request Cuchullain had made sure the son would refuse.

In the tale, Cuchullain's only child bears his mother's name. He is called Condla, son of the warrior goddess Aife. In the story known as "The Death of Aife's Son," Cuchullain's wife Emer recognizes the boy and advises his father:

> Do not slaughter your son, impetuous, well-bred lad. Neither fair nor right [is it]. Turn away from the skin-torment of the sapling of your tree. . . . Turn to me! . . .
>
> But Cuchullain answers, "Silence Woman! It is not a woman's advice I seek regarding deeds of bright splendour. Such deeds are not performed with a woman's assistance. Let us be triumphant in feats. Sated the eyes of a great king. A mist of blood upon my skin from the gore of the body of Condla. "
>
> . . . . [After the lad nearly beats him, he] deceived the boy with the *gae bolga*, [his unique spear trick that always causes mortal wounds]. Then he took the boy in his arms and carried him from the

---

[66] In the battle manual of the terrorist highjackers of 9/11, the men were warned not to become swept away, to remember that all they did, including the sacrificial slaughter of victims who resisted them, and their own suicides, was to honor the god of their people.

shore and showed him to the Ulaid [his tribe] saying, "Here is my son, men of Ulster."

"Alas, indeed" they said . . . [and] cries of grief were raised, and his [Condla's] grave and marker were made and for three days not a calf of the cows of . . . [Ulster] was left alive after him.[67]

The ritual slaughter of the calves mirrors the ritual killing of Condla. Reminding us of the sacrifice of Isaac and the massacre of the innocents that also ushered in a new era, the killings of the son of the goddess and the calves of the milchers provide a terrible foundation ritual for a new phase of Irish culture.

The emerging father principle, to further its one-sidedly masculine cause, demands the sacrifice of the son of the mother. The killing of the goddess's child serves to disparage her powers and the father's previous equal participation with her in conception and parenting. Earlier in his story, Cuchullain had held his sword against Aife and demanded that she give him a son. We are to understand that the goddess is no longer the sovereign chooser of her own partners and the bestower of the gifts of life. Her acquiescence to the warrior's threat and her son's slaughter symbolize the movement of Cuchullain's people away from their embeddedness in the revered matrix and toward reverence of masculine heroism and domination. The male warrior claims powers over life and death hitherto ascribed equally to the goddess and her partner. While Cuchullain's act is dreadful, for his time it is perhaps culturally necessary in order to establish the patrifocal era.

To fulfill his role as harbinger of this new era, the warrior destroys the fruit of his own paternity. Through this sacrifice he channels the personal libido, which would naturally have gone into the process of his fathering of the lad, toward the archetypal father principle and to the "great king" and community of males who rule now in the god's name.[68]

Expressing the increasing movement of Bronze Age patrifocal

---

[67] Jeffrey Gantz, ed. and trans., *Early Irish Myths and Sagas,* pp. 150ff.

[68] Cf. Rene Girard, *Violence and the Sacred.*

culture toward heroic individualism, which can sacrifice as well as guard the great gift of life, Cuchullain proves his place with the men of Ulster. As their ever-youthful champion, he represents force separated from fathering. This results in his remaining a particular kind of eternal youth. He serves his adolescent self-aggrandizement through embodying the heroic ideals of the collective that separate him from caretaking his own life and that of his child. He valiantly guards the lands and herds of Ulster, but not his own son.

As a result, Cuchullain does not have to experience inner conflict between his warrior and paternal roles, between self-assertion and compassion, or between power and need. He simply destroys one side of the potential ambivalence. Psychologically this leaves him without the problem of sustaining inner conflict. And this, in turn, prevents his experiencing himself as the ground on which opposing drives can play and battle. Without learning to hold and suffer contradictions, he never has to achieve an internalized sense of individuality.

We can see a similar pattern today in the ever-youthful men who have failed to develop beyond their heroic phase. They represent the remnant of a culture that is waning, for today we find ever-increasing numbers of young fathers who are remarkably attuned with, and participate in, child rearing. While warrior fathers may biologically produce children to prove their potency, they often fail in their parenting tasks, just as Cuchullain did. Through denial of paternal responsibility, which they have often not experienced adequately from their own fathers, they may evade monetary and psychological support for the children they consider the mother's. Remaining identified with their heroic role at work, they may become obsessed with proving themselves against peers, so they are not able to relate compassionately. At home they may become competitive and envious toward their children. We might say they manifest a kind of desperate, manic, phallic defense against experiencing their own vulnerability and/or their grief at the intolerable loss of a balanced parental archetype in their own life. They suffer the severe narcissistic wounds of a one-sided, patrifocal culture.

Just as he scorns his wife in relation to his son, Cuchullain also spurns the great earth and war goddess Morrigan. He can only honor her after he has rejected her advances and offer of help. In response, she becomes competitive, and they spar verbally. She threatens that she will become an adversary. When he is most pressed by his foes in battle, she comes against him in three animal forms. He proves his might by wounding her each time. But later, when Cuchullain is exhausted and needs to regain the goddess's bounty to fight on, she assumes the form of an old woman who offers him milk. Then he blesses her. The three blessings heal the wounds he has inflicted. Once restored, he regrets having given them. The sequential oppositions within the warrior obscure Cuchullain's awareness of his conflicting drives. We see an analogous pattern in adolescent psychology, exemplified in rejection of the devalued and still needed mother.

In the older mythology of the Dagda, the relationship between genders is far less polarized and does not require a male's defensive disdain of the female to prove his superiority or gain individuality. It does not require destruction of the primary bonds to the matrix of life, nor a sacrifice of the child to ensure domination of its vulnerabilities, which are then identified with the feminine. Neither does it diminish the male.

When the Dagda meets the great Morrigan, standing with her feet across the river Unshin and washing the nine long tresses of her hair, he greets her. Then he "conversed with her, and they made a union"[69] that they both wanted. The partnership is equal, mutually respectful and passionate. Thus the modern sculptor Michael Quirke depicts the goddess as part of the Dagda's figure, standing directly and intimately behind the god. From the loving union, the Dagda gained the Morrigan's help in battle, and the landscape itself gained its double name—"The Bed of the Couple" and "The Ford of Destruction." Love and death, joining and separating, are marked here as equally valid transitions in the greater life process that the

---

[69] Gray, *Cath Maige Tuired,* p. 45.

old god serves with the goddess.

By contrast, Cuchullain seeks his own enduring fame above all. He spurns the goddess's aid as if it would only diminish his glory. Unlike the Dagda, he can only relate to the feminine through domination, lust, competition, depression and finally death. Yet, for this phallic-aggressive, still beardless, omnipotent warrior, physical survival is irrelevant. Cuchullain takes up arms on a day destined to grant him great renown albeit a short life. Like modern suicide bombers, the early Irish warrior believes he will live on to enjoy wine, women, music and war in the Celtic Land of the Ever-Living, the Land over the Waves. More importantly, his honor will live forever in the memory of his tribe as long as the poets praise his great deeds. To this end, Cuchullain glories in exhibitionism and lets no challenge pass without valiantly overcoming it. Yet he still does not believe he has achieved all he might. Like Hercules, he finds that his greatest adversary is the goddess, who also forces him to his great unique feats.

While Cuchullain represents a vital stage in the creation of the heroic style of ego, his material exposes some of the motives for war and domination of the earth—motives that Ervin Laszlo calls those of conquest, colonization and consumption.[70] On the other hand, Cuchullain's stories provide useful orientation in clinical work with clients emerging into mastery, struggling with the narcissism that cannot yield to frighteningly uncontrolled potentials and working through midlife crises when heroic, power-driven accomplishment finally falls flat.

He lives on. We glimpse him as a story gift from his alcoholic father to young Frank McCourt.[71] He stares us down in the tribal clashes in Ulster, the former Yugoslavia, Africa and the Middle East. We know him in ourselves when our identity is threatened by an adversary or problem. Since the youthful, aggressive warrior represents the principle of competitive striving and the guardianship

---

[70] Laszlo, lecture at Assisi Conference, August 2000.
[71] See McCourt, *Angela's Ashes*.

of values that his group considers sacred, we can also find plenty of contemporary equivalents. We can read about them on commuter train posters extolling corporate battlers who serve the bottom line. We also see them in the news serving ideals of democracy, perverted and greedy individualism, or *jihad.*

The archetypal warrior learns how to overcome adversaries and survive, and also how to face the fear of what has been considered the inevitable and unspeakable adversary, the end of life.[72] In ancient Irish lore this was called knowing the way of the black ravens, those carrion eaters of the battlefield that represent the triple goddess Morrigan. While the Dagda is her partner, himself an immortal lord of life and death, later heroes, such as Cuchullain, Beowulf and Gawain go forth with increasing consciousness of their own mortality to earn their epic songs of praise.

We can see that the hero, a warrior extolled by the collective, may be a terrorist on a holy mission seeking praise at home and celestial virgins in heaven, a soldier in Vietnam or Bosnia, a freedom fighter in France, Alabama or Chechnya, an altruist hiding victims in a holocaust, an aid worker in Afghanistan, a scaler of the world's highest mountains or a young woman living in a redwood tree. Our endorsements vary according to our own perspective on the adversary and our ideals. Thus the same warrior can be both enemy and hero, as Russia's premier Vladimir Putin so clearly expressed on National Public Radio when he spoke of the novelist Solzhenitzen—once branded an enemy by the restrictive NKVD that employed Putin himself—as now being a heroic spokesperson for emerging values.

It is the partisan need to split an issue into opposing perspectives

---

[72] Death in this culture that overvalues material well-being, youthful bodies and personal success is split from spirit and transcendence. It has often been a tabooed subject, although the coverage of the World Trade Center disaster and the Afghan war have changed this somewhat. In general a majority of doctors prefer not to deal with death in speaking with dying patients. In group therapy with cancer patients, some therapists may even forbid clients to discuss it together as too depressing.

that marks the warrior, whether she or he is a protagonist striking out against repressive structures of power, or an adversary of newer forms of consciousness. Striving against another in the service of old or emerging collective ideals makes the warrior. The ideal itself may be the strength to reach the top and dominate. On an extroverted level, heroic service raises shadow issues of righteousness, hypocrisy and naive pacifism for those who would do good, and issues of the fraudulent seizing of power for personal aggrandizement for those who forge ahead and destroy. It also raises issues of what Jungians call shadow projection, for we know that what we do not see within ourselves, we see only too well in others. When we devalue and scorn our enemy for manifesting certain values and qualities, we know we invariably also need to pause and look within to discover how we handle those values and qualities in ourselves.

On an inner level, we can see that heroic service is required to overcome old loyalties that enmesh us in patterns that run counter to our becoming more of what we are destined to be. When we experience the eruption of fear, grief or rage, as when we are threatened by outer events or move toward a commitment to the Self, we may soften, but more often we flee or fight. As we struggle against transformation in the service of what we are identified with, we may find warriors and the terror of death on both sides within ourselves. Thus we can have inner warriors engaging in what the prophet Mohammed called the true, inner *jihad*. Jung points to conscious engagement in this inner battle as an antidote to externalized conflict:

> The whole world with its turmoil and misery is in an individuation process. But people don't know it, that's the only difference. If they knew it, they would not be at war with each other, because whoever has the war inside himself has no time and pleasure to fight others.[73]

There are long stretches of analytic work where such inner con-

---

[73] See Jung, *Letters*, vol. 1, p. 442 (25 Sept., 1946).

flict rages back and forth. Softening may ultimately be necessary, but premature softening is a loss. And the wisdom to know the right moment is often very difficult. Thus the Grail question for King Arthur's knights of the Round Table becomes ethically crucial for us today: What do you (and your striving) serve? It is not easy to find and walk the path that serves the life process in its many changing permutations.

On this path we may sometimes even be forced, like Arjuna in the Bhagavad-Gita, but hopefully not in what would now be the self-serving way of Cuchullain, to destroy what we hold dear when it stands in the way of the unfolding of our destiny and that of history itself. Distinguishing between the true requirements of our fated calling and indulgence in narcissistic envy, rote obedience or fanaticism is very difficult. The choice depends on our capacity to be conscious and sustain the conflicting voices within until we can sort out their messages. Hence it depends on psychological development. Increasingly today we find such decisions are an issue of conscience, the inner voice that attunes us with the individual Self. Heeding its call rather than leaping to obey emotional impulse and/or collective, superego injunctions presents ever-painful conflicts that become central in psychotherapy as in life.

On an introverted level, the drive to be "mighty in battle" like the Dagda is part of our struggle toward a more unified personality. It is an early and necessary step toward asserting our wholeness in reaction to opposition. Hence we need to acknowledge that we are gifted with aggression and programmed by biology and culture to seek mastery in order to preserve ourselves and what we hold dear. We are also programmed to identify ourselves in terms of similarities to, and differences from, others and ourselves. Our family, gender, group and god begin to be learned in infancy when we discriminate strangers from those who are known.

It is not far from this type of pattern recognition to ethnic, gender, class, age and religious profiling. The persons we know best are valued most. We stay loyal to them to survive on their terms for much or even all of our lives. We thus tend to define the boundaries and forms of our group as arbiters of our security even when they may be sources of misery. Many times a client has told me that he or she has to put biological family ties and duties ahead of needs for a deeper, better fit with a kindred soul or group. "Only my family will always be there," explains one woman mortally afraid of feeling abandoned. Or another complains, "I cannot go my own way or speak my own perceptions; I will be too lonely."

Trust is initially bound up in biological kin and in social or religious group. Few such groups in our culture teach that we are kin to other tribes or species. Thus alongside of the current paradigmatic shift toward affiliation with the deep structures that support a new kind of interdependence and integration, we still harbor tribally instilled urges that make us perceive and cling to our identity with familiar, seemingly sacred but often superficial differences. These motivate our internal warrior to guard the boundaries beyond which we fear to go, boundaries that open to the new and unknown. Inevitably then, we resist our own transformation because we shall have to face disloyalty and disorientation, both from others and in our own depths. The parts of us in thrall to familiar authorities battle against claiming all we might become. "Abandon your father and mother and follow Me," says the Christian representative of the Self, but we are too often prevented from opening toward the holism that we and our culture need to embrace.

Every time one client began to open toward creative energy, he fled back to obsessive practicalities. Another experienced her habitual inner critic attacking all her attempts to draw the images of her dreams. Because of our loyalty to such familiar patterns, we often experience the energy pressing us toward transformation as an annihilating enemy—like the angel of his blessing that the Biblical Jacob fought so desperately. (Gen. 32:24-32) Yet also like that angel, it can be the initiating agent that forces us to claim our potential strength even as we battle it. And indeed its purpose is to show us the limits of our current identity.

The image of the warrior provides us with an orientation with which to face our deepest issues of vulnerability as we develop the courage to claim the warrior's powers. But just as our infant selves needed a buffer from unthinkable anxieties, so as adults we need containers and companions to help us to relate to such assaults. Otherwise and understandably, we may defend against over-whelming helplessness with primitive denial, with splitting and projection, or with giving in too soon and identifying with the ag-gressor, hoping to survive. These are dynamics from magic struc-tures of consciousness that attempt to control chaos and the terror of annihilation.

The defense of separating from and ejecting psychological mate-rial that we cannot bear has been coming into my mind a lot in re-lation to the current "war" against terrorism. In September 2001, President George W. Bush simplistically challenged nations to be "for us or against us" when he said they had to choose "either free-dom or terror." Nonetheless, many of us also feel anxiety about a response to terrorism on its own level that seems to be colluding with the purpose of the terrible, goading attacks and the escalation inherent in such struggles. Its one-sidedness can usurp our poten-tials to look more deeply and find solutions that may be less excit-ing but ultimately more life-enhancing.

The Extreme Warrior

Terrorist attacks have given us a new image for the extreme war-rior. Glorying in destruction and the honors of martyrdom, the sui-cidal terrorist baits us into an either/or polarization, warrior against warrior, ideal against ideal. Motivated by destructive envy mixed with desires for fame on earth and eternal reward in heaven, the terrorist is as fearless as Cuchullain. Unlike the early warrior, he may not depend on possession by wild beserker energy, but he is pledged to the same ruthless destruction. Without capacity for dia-logue or any concern for holism, this warrior also lurks in us to de-fend the old power-based authorities that resist transformation.

Not surprisingly many clients began to use the image of the ter-rorist as a metaphor for issues that arose in their own responses to the attacks of 9/11 and since then. One fragile borderline woman came her into session identified with terrorism and spewing vengeance, although she would have been horrified to recognize her possession. She ranted that "all Muslims should be sent home." Slowly we found the terror and helplessness in her and discovered that the emotions resonated with early experiences of victimization by an uncle who was a European immigrant. Silenced then, she could finally find her own voice and begin both to value its passion and to release her consciousness from blind identity with either the victim or the aggressor.[74] The rage, given its proper context, helped to coalesce her fragile, terrified ego. This represented a primal step toward developing a capacity to value and guard her own identity. Sometimes she could glimpse her projection of the uncle onto all tan-skinned persons, but for many months she remained hesitant to get into a taxi without a companion.

A man recognized his inner terrorist when he noticed that he wanted to allow his very young son to watch the repeated TV images of the planes attacking the World Trade Center towers, "because," as he said, "the boy needs to feel some realistic fear." Having protected his son from the deprivation and horrors of his own childhood, he was himself very upset when his own terror erupted to resonate with the destruction in New York. With horror and shame, he realized he was acting out an attack of envy, recognizing that the deprived part of him even wanted to subtly endanger his son's greater sense of security. Fortunately he caught himself before he acted out something akin to Cuchullain's slaughter of Condla.

A colleague confessed that she wanted to kick a friend, because he had been called to volunteer in a hospital and she hadn't. What she later called her "inner terrorist" leapt to start a competitive war. Several traumatized clients woke in panic in the night wondering what was next, reliving the scenes of falling buildings and jumping

---

[74] Synchronistically, on the way to a session, she passed a chalk statement written on the sidewalk by the local street artist, de la Vega. It said, "An eye for an eye and the whole world's blind."

humans, suffering strong survivor guilt. They began to identify their terror as an inner attacker, magnifying their fears. In each instance they were eventually able to link the extreme emotions in the current crisis with similarly structured early experiences of abuse and an introjected, terrorizing aggressor. "The planes . . . [were] like my drunk father throwing furniture," said one woman who had spent her life in hiding and her career caring for foster children onto whom she could project her vulnerability.[75] She had never been able to assert herself, because she could not differentiate assertion from abuse.

In therapy, the shadow figures of the extreme warrior and the threatening, outmoded, fundamentalist ideals that sustain the terrorist (called "my inner Taliban," by one client) can begin to be worked with to move the emotions and energies toward consciousness. Several individuals, who usually identified with the victims in their psyche, found the courage to resist patterns of inner abuse when they could see the need for an inner struggle against the complexes impeding their development.

The Dagda Model of Warrior

I witnessed a remarkable confrontation with a potentially terrorist shadow that occurred in a single session with a man who had been working at Ground Zero in New York. He came in to talk on day ten only because he was upset and angry that his wife was "falling apart, constantly crying and fearful . . . [and] she wouldn't get a grip." He wondered if she needed hospitalization. Projecting the qualities of "weak and emotional," he identified with the ideals of his stern, macho superego. He described himself as "a tough guy who gets up everyday and does his work," a "soldier" like his dad and Vietnam veteran uncle. In the session, however, he acknowledged that holding to his ego ideal had made him, even as a boy, ashamed to admit vulnerability and suffering. In psychological

---

75 Cf. Perera, "War, Madness, and the Morrigan: A Celtic Goddess of Life and Death."

terms, he had dissociated from such painful emotions out of a long habit that now served well to enable him to do his grueling work. The emotions didn't vanish, however. He had cut them off like a good warrior and projected them onto his wife.

This man courageously began to realize that "she is feeling [the grief and fear] for both of us." Knowing that he didn't want his wife "to have to carry all of it," he opened to his share of the emotional burden and found with surprise and a big sigh that he was relieved. Before he left, he confessed quietly that he had, while watching TV alone at night, "let a few tears fall for the families of the dead." I was filled with respect for the loving heart that had helped him to see and work with more of his own emotional fullness in order to grow softer and more expansive toward himself and his partner.

Following September 2001, many New Yorkers have honored and been grateful to the workers at Ground Zero. Firemen, police and construction crew members have spoken of the ways they have tried to manage the emotional stress in order to shield their families. Over the months, they have been faced with a task few warriors in our country have ever had. After each shift fighting to clear the rubble and body parts, they had to return to families who they sought to protect from the horrors they were confronting. While this is not so different from the requirements normally demanded of nurses, doctors, police, firefighters and other caretakers, the scale and duration have received unusual media attention. It has been important for us all to empathize with the usually hidden side of the warriors—their tears at work, their nightmares and bad moods at home, and their felt needs to stay apart from family to spare those they love while they try to cope.

Such complexity and capacities for expansiveness have made me think of the Dagda. Described as "the swift Dagda [who] was deadly as a poison draught," he is also "a just dealing lord over the feast"—the king's feast at which all the different factions assemble together to celebrate the life of their larger community.[76] Thus, like

---

[76] Gwynn, *The Metrical Dindschenchas,* p. 93

those workers, while the ancient Dagda is a great battler, he is also much more. His capacity to guard and stand against adversaries is complemented by other functions to rule over, take in, submit, nurture, express emotions, heal and join together.

In this ancient figure we can see reflected the new ideal of hero that we are discovering we need to honor in those serving life as they also clear the destruction at Ground Zero and other war-torn sites around the world.

5

Integration Through Regal Functions:
Earthy Virility and Just Order

The figure of the Dagda represents diverse aspects of the life process. As warrior, he stands strongly and courageously against adversaries in order to guard the values and reality of the life process. However, he is also described as "King in Erin . . . a prince, noble, slender."[77] This means that he functions within a larger context than the Bronze Age hero. The Dagda, as a ruler himself and as the deity behind early kingship in Ireland, represents embodied fertility and the ability to encompass and hold together opposing factions in a just, thriving, and holistic balance. Against foe, he might be a warrior, but in relation to the diversity within or when claiming rule over the tribes of a new territory, he had to balance and make its parts work together creatively. The mark of a just Irish king was his ability to see the deep truth in any situation and use it as his guide when there was a conflict of interests.

Fertility

An ancient chief was considered the temporary consort of the goddess of the land. It was said that when he was virile and generous, the goddess bestowed her bounty on the earth, so the tribe could thrive. Then poets praised the ruler. These fertility functions of the Dagda as ruler are consistent with his bull form.

As bull god, the Dagda has power over herds and milk production. Worshipped also as grain and fruit, he ensures bountiful harvests. He owns two ever-bearing fruit trees and two marvelous swine, one of which is always being cooked, the other always alive.[78] He controls the weather and its effects on the harvest, and with his harp he strums the seasons in fruitful order all year.

---

77 Gwynn, *The Metrical Dindschenchas*, p. 103.
78 O hOgain, *Myth, Legend and Romance*, p. 274.

Although called the good god because he is functionally good at everything, the Dagda himself is not a beauty. Far earthier than the aristocratic later Celts like Cuchullain, who were proud of their good looks and elegant attire, he cares more for the lusty, physical pleasures of sex and eating and working than for appearances. This earns him the titles "Beautiful One" and "Source" from the earth goddess. Nonetheless, to emphasize the fact that he represents a devalued earlier era, the Irish storytellers gloried in pointing out his distance from their noble aesthetic ideal. They described the Dagda as an ugly giant, a peasant bumpkin from the edges of culture. A modern scholar explains,

> He bear[s] the stamp of a primitive style which redactors have delib-
> erately pressed to a grotesque extreme. Hideous and potbellied, he
> wears a cowl and a short tunic like that of the Gaulish god of the
> mallet; . . . in Irish sagas long garments are a measure of the dignity
> of the wearer, and his tunic is the ordinary attire of churls. His boots
> are of horsehide with the hair outside, like the shoes of rawhide still
> worn today [that was 1940] by the fishermen of the western [Irish]
> islands.[79]

Burly and gutsy, this earthy Dagda has a huge penis and no problems using it. He mates with various goddesses to enjoy consensual sex, to enlist their help for his tribe, and to produce children. The Dagda is not merely a spiritual father but a sensate, begetting father of daughters and sons. The Cerne Abbas Giant, carved into a hillside in Dorset, England, is a figure reminiscent of the Dagda, with his obvious capacity for phallic potency (opposite). Into the early twentieth century, barren couples used to sleep in the penis sculpted on this hillside in the hope of becoming fertile. Above the figure on the hill is an earthwork of concentric rectangles where the May pole was raised for the traditional rites, revels, games and amorous liaisons.[80]

---

[79] Sjoestedt, *Gods and Heroes,* pp. 53f.
[80] Whitlock, *In Search of Lost Gods,* p. 112.

The Cerne Abbas Giant.
(From *The Tourist Guide to Dorset*)

Such creative masculine power supports life. It appears in modern clinical practice in both women's and men's material when the instinctual base of life has been feared and repressed with overly intellectual and controlling defenses. In most instances, images of a lusty Dagda-like figure appear in a woman's material after she has a sense that the feminine body-ego has acquired enough earthy support from the Self to relate positively to such a fully embodied and respectful masculinity.

GL

I think of one remarkably creative client whose mother had treated her like a Barbie doll to be dressed up and fussed at, and who had taught her that she could dim the lights by putting the plug only half way into the socket. She was too bright at age three to fall for that, but she was very afraid of intensity and had chosen not to become a mother herself. Her boyish father's favorite experiences revolved around squiring his wife and children to Sunday dinner at his mother's house. Not surprisingly she had had many sexual encounters with "nice and safe" men who were passive, identified with their intellects, or sexually interested in other men. Her husband was all of these. When I first met her, she was overly intellectual, a resentful caretaker, and anxiously focused on her body, so every extra ounce felt like the onset of obesity, every twinge a sign of cancer.

After several years of analysis in which she worked with many aspects of her mother complex, she had a series of dreams bringing her a new sense of the masculine and her own potential depth. In the first, she dreamt of a man who was returning from overseas. He was so unknown, she couldn't even imagine him. Then in another dream she saw the returning man as a tall, homeless foreigner who might be "a drug dealer or shaman." A few weeks later he reappeared as a burly handyman who was caring of animals but not very bright. Then he appeared as a large woman with deep cleavage who turned out to be a man in drag.

As she claimed more of her own value and natural sexuality (imaged in one dream as the gift of a new red skirt to wear to a dance from "a woman who follows the white cow"), she dreamed that a handsome, muscular dairy farmer had been given another job as a mailman—spelled inadvertently in her dream journal as "m-a-l-e." In the dream this caretaker of cows helps her find her way home by pointing to the position of the stars in the Big Dipper. The man reminded her of a boyfriend from college with whom she had gone on a brief canoeing trip. She regretted that she had not then been able to receive his loving appreciation of her and her body. A few months later a similar dream figure appeared in the lobby of her yoga class as a kind of mountain man playing with a frisky, three-legged dog. He invites her to go out with him, and, feeling conflicted, she wakes up. Identifying with the animal's woundedness as she told the dream, she wept. Later she explained:

> The man lives off the grid. He's not interested in social conventions. I guess he can accept the raw reality of life and death and even his dog's woundedness so it doesn't have to feel ashamed.

There are many parallels in this sequence of images to our *Dagda Mor*. The figure is initially unknown and homeless in her psychology. Slowly her dreams reveal him to be related to issues of altered consciousness, caring for animals, earthiness, androgyny, masculinity, astronomy, deep appreciation of the feminine, and non-shaming empathy for vulnerability.

On the other hand, this kind of earthy potency may seem initially dangerous to a modern Victorian. It was thus imaged in a dream of a woman struggling with the antilibidinous, controlling superego of her family. This negative animus had driven her far from the sources of a many-sided creative potential and damaged her relation to archetypal drive patterns. Both the energies of desire and assertion were trapped. She came into therapy in a serious, self-loathing depression. Nearly a year later she dreamt:

> I am on the bus coming to therapy, sitting next to a huge man. He looks like a bum, really messy, with rough hair and ratty clothes and an ugly stick. He even has an animal in his lap. I wonder how the bus driver let him on. I worry that he smells. Then I notice that he wears a thick, gold, snaky necklace that looks very valuable. I worry

more because I am sure he stole it. I start to look for another seat, but my little boy climbs over to him and climbs up as if he were a tree, to sit on his shoulders. I worry that his diaper is wet. The man doesn't seem to mind and smiles.

In the dream, she meets a new, very Dagda-like animus, complete with a Celtic golden torque. She described the man's energy as "slow, still and huge—the opposite of me." But he is also messy, sensuous, even aromatic, and instinctive. Sitting next to the figure of the bum feels dangerous and full of "worry" to her tidy ideals. Yet, like the tree of life, he can comfortably support her free, peeing, self-expressing child, her own future growth.

The Dagda well represents the powers of this bum, although I did not tell the dreamer about him. Not only did I know little about Celtic mythology at that point, but I felt that speaking about mythic symbolism was premature since so much of the dream is on a body level—smells, excretion, mess, activity. The child part of her is comfortable with this and initiates a friendly relationship. However, mythological amplification or even rational interpretation carries here the threat of switching to other kinds of consciousness and robbing her of the excited beginnings of her own embodied creative process. The figure represents what Jung calls "coming events still hidden in the archetypal realm."[81] The energies are distant from her usual awareness and still ringed with anxiety.

We explored how she was meeting this earthy energy in personal life. Her association to "worry [about] . . . smells" was to using my waiting room bathroom the previous week. Brought up to run the water as she peed and to burn matches to erase her body odors, she had been so eager to start the session that she had forgotten to do her usual cover-up. We explored her fear that she was "so disgusting" she would have to stop the therapy. Then, because I know that smells are connected with the first chakra in Kundalini yoga, *muladhara,* which carries the energies of primary, earthy incarnation,

---

[81]*Letters,* vol. 2, p. 616. Elsewhere Jung writes of "the creative psychic background" of the archetype (ibid., p. 606).

and the child in the dream was accepted by the masculine figure, I asked her to tell me about the little boy. She had trouble imagining the child, inhibited by the shame she carried from her own childhood. With some urging she thought, "It is a boy about one year old." I wondered aloud about what had happened a year ago, and she noted with surprise that that was when she had begun analysis.

I thought to myself that in many ways she was still on the bus, on her way into the treatment, not yet in analysis. Usually she even resisted talking about her history, saying she remembered nothing important, but now when I asked about herself at one year, she felt able to say with pride based on an accomplishment that did not match the wet, climbing baby that she was "fully toilet trained by one year," just before the birth of a favored sibling. The confluence of those events suggested that she had experienced a demand for premature bodily control and separation from the mother at the same time. The emotional residue of these events had still to be consciously experienced and transformed in the course of therapy, but she was able to begin to consider the anxieties about embodiment that she had carried through life.

Even though she feared and devalued him consciously, the bum's appearance on the bus to her analytic session reassured me that she was anxiously but deeply involved and at least well on the way to therapy. The woman herself usually had a good cover-up, a seriously impenetrable persona. She often appeared to be coming to sessions out of a detached, very reasonable sense of duty that was allowing her to forego medication. She talked about things in a very quiet, bland voice and was often politely critical of herself and me, "helpfully" noticing when there was a dead leaf on a plant in the office or that the colors I was wearing were or were not the ones recommended by a book she used. She experienced her comments as friendly and appropriate, the way she recalled that her parents had cared for their daughters.

As I thought about the archetypal image and began discovering the fullness of the Dagda mythologem, I sensed the potentials in the client's psyche that might become available to consciousness. Perhaps some intuition of that had made me more patient toward the devaluing judgmental complex that slashed deftly at me and sought to keep her from opening to her emotions.

The Dagda stands for a state of equilibrium prior to, though including, differentiation. For many of us, he can represent a sense of wholeness that we may achieve after we have begun to accept our infantile shadow and relate to its archetypal emotions. This process that we often call regression can also be forward looking, for it forces us to reclaim and integrate the ever-broadening range of potential that individuation requires. The timing of the dream in this client's process suggested that her psyche was opening to the possibilities of such a regression, finding a sturdy enough, new kind of accepting masculine spirit.

Balanced Opposites

The Dagda himself holds *yang* and *yin* energies in balance to convey an image of the full masculine. His special emblems are the wooden club and a cauldron. We know these motifs from ancient India as *lingam* and *yoni*, god and goddess. They reappear in Arthurian legend as lance and grail, in the Tarot cards as wands and cups. Together they represent the male and female implements of ritual magic, just as they are the male and female organs of sexuality in the body. Or what Genia Haddon calls the phallic and testicular, assertive and receptive aspects of the masculine.[82]

The term used for the club in the text is *lorg*. It has a cluster of meanings in Old Irish, and, as is common in the tales, all of them infuse the myth. *Lorg* means cudgel, stick, wand of office; mark, track, path and penis. With the rough end of his *lorg*, the Dagda can kill nine warriors. With the other, smooth end, he can restores nine to life. This great phallic club is both a weapon and a healing wand. Symbolizing the effective assertion needed for mastery, it is an instrument of practical and magical powers, including destruction, authority, creativity and healing. It represents the Dagda's powers

---

[82] Haddon, *Uniting Sex, Self and Spirit.*

as master of life and death, and of the continual cycle of destruction and creation that underlie the dynamic maintenance of individuals and the cosmos.

In a modern man's dream such vital masculine power was imaged as a shape-shifting penis. The dreamer was struggling to retrieve his buried artistic potential, to end a marriage in which he was emotionally and physically abused, and to come to terms with his homoeroticism. He dreamt:

> A man like my maternal uncle tells me he will show me something. He pulls out his huge penis. It is also somehow a wolf and a bird. It's erect and seems dangerous. "You have one too," he tells me.

The uncle was a man the dreamer was close to at age four. The dreamer described him as a loud, tough, warm fellow, whom he later learned was scorned by his intellectually pretentious, alcoholic father. Following the model his father preferred, the dreamer repudiated those qualities and his own earthy masculinity. The dream shows that he cannot believe he has such phallic power himself. He cannot identify with male potency. Nonetheless, he had collaborated in eliciting a brutal animus in his wife and currently felt compelled to pursue men whom he came to recognize, as we discussed this dream, were like his uncle.

While he craved such partners, he also despised them and was fearful of intimate relationships with them. Instead, he made his body dangerously available to whomever might desire transient sex, as if he were nothing but an anal receptacle or a penis to be aroused by another man's attentions. He actually did not see himself as a whole or autonomous person but as a series of discontinuous states. Thus he could allow any man who wanted them to take his body parts as fetishes. These passive encounters provided him with moments of exciting enlivenment. Addicted to servicing another's needs because he had a "good body," he gained an illusory sense of value and a superficial sense of relatedness that kept him going back to the gay baths and steam rooms.

The dream figure and the animals represent aspects of Self energy he needed to claim for himself, and their appearance in such shape-shifting form implied the potential of his opening to the process of transformation.[83] The wolf, he said, "might be a loner and hungry, even aggressive. Oh no, I remember now: wolves mark their territory and mate for life." Later he mused, "The bird is a raptor. It goes for [and] seizes what it needs. . . . Well, I don't even know what I want. That's too confusing. I let the person have his needs." He said this as if he himself was clearly not such a person in the equation.

This man expected the other to reenact the authority and contempt he had experienced from his parents, and he was deeply conflicted about claiming such phallic-aggressive potential. It felt, he said, "unChristian," rationalizing his masochistic victimization. Nonetheless, the figure of the Dagda-like man with his big, animal and bird, penis horn represents the primary, chthonic and spiritual masculinity he both craves in others and fears to own for himself as both penetrating power and passion for union. It encompasses the instinctual aggression and spirit required to honor desirousness and self-esteem. It is the kind a boy of four, as the dreamer was when he was still close to his uncle, would need in order to empower his fuller development and enable commitment to his own potential wholeness and to responsible, deeper relationships.

An elderly, very creative, gentle woman who had lost her husband was faced with claiming the potentials for independence and poetic voice that he had expressed for them both. These qualities, which she valued but felt she could not manifest, had been curtailed by a scornful, devaluing superego with which she had struggled throughout her life. She dreamed:

A rough giant, dressed in short animal skins, comes into a hall where I am. The hall has many closed doors, and he begins to knock them open with a tree trunk he holds. I am annoyed. He doesn't care what people think about him so he can do what he wants.

---

[83] See Perera, "Samain and Self: Uncanny Images of Transformation."

She drew the figure and discovered that the tree trunk has "a smooth end and a jagged one," nearly replicating the old description of the ends of the Dagda's club. The figure's vitality and boorish behavior compensated her sense of herself and frightened her with its "uncaring self-indulgence." His powerful, bivalent club also suggested that both destructive and revitalizing energies would be needed for the psychological work to be done.

Another clinical example of the club, also illuminating its capacity to embody the balanced energy of the opposites, came in a man's dream:

> I go into a cellar, then into the sub-basement, where I have never been before, to get something. I am with an unknown woman. As I am looking around, a tiger appears out of the shadows. I am terrified. But the woman points to an old table where there is a huge, ancient pair of blunt shears. By holding the handles so the blades are together, I point at the tiger and hold it at bay while we carefully back up the stairs. I close the door and bolt it with incredible relief.

Much later he recalled this "tiger in the cellar dream" when he dreamt of a similar image:

> I use a pair of blunt shears in the garden to prune the dead branches out of a tree I have planted.

This man was a recovering alcoholic often possessed by savage, tigerish outbreaks of unmitigated aggression when he drank. In the previous therapy session, he had not realized how angry he had been when I ended the session on time even though he had been unavoidably late. However, instead of succumbing to the "pure, uncaring, wild rage," which he associated to the tiger, and failing to show up for his next session, as he often had, he came with the dream.

The unknown woman reminded him of a caring friend. Her appearance here as an aspect of his inner world tells us that he was beginning to care about his own psychological process as it goes into the cellar's depths. We can also see the female figure as a suggestion of the therapist who expressed care for him through her protection of the discipline and boundaries of his analytic work. Having an experience of caring companionship to balance his identity with the aggressive drive energy, the dreamer could experience the symbol of the shears as a means of holding the opposites together. Single-pointed, it could allow him to set limits against acting out the raw tiger energy and gain the power of willed, intentional action.[84]

Rather than killing off the tiger, because dissociation is neither possible nor desirable, the dream presented the dreamer with an image of a crafted tool to set limits against the full expression of threatening instinctual rage. The blades of the shears themselves suggest the cutting destruction that engenders shape when opposing forces collide creatively. Here they are held together to form a staff with which to focus energy and set a limit that can help the dreamer toward the healing of his addictive outbursts.

From the depths of his unconscious, the image of the blunt shears was like the gift of the essence of the aggressive and healing powers of the Dagda's club. When he was later trying to clarify a new potential in his psyche, his subsequent dream returned the image to consciousness as a differentiating tool. At that point he was beginning to work consciously with his conflicting emotions. In both of his images, we can see the potential gradient of phallic aggressive energy. He became able to bear the struggle of opposing energies. In their very conflict he gained an awareness of himself as an inner battleground. This becomes the landscape of the inner kingdom, and starts him on the path toward claiming the club as the staff of authority and self-rule.

While the Dagda's cudgel is too gross an image for contemporary science, it is the grandparent of one of the most modern tools of discrimination. Our subtle laser technology—the weapon of

---

[84] Cuchullain's ritual of exit from his initiatory rage involved a similar confrontation of the aggressive drive with caring, empathic support. See Perera. "Ritual Integration of Aggression in Psychotherapy."

light—carries the same potential to kill and/or heal. The image of the Dagda's club also helps me deal with borderline levels in analysands. Remembering it, I can usually hold both sides of the polarized emotions that erupt as frantic extremes.

One client comes to mind. In some sessions she was full of envious hate and abuse. Sometimes we could later trace her rage to some wound she experienced as coming from me or in another relationship she was placing in the transference to me. In other sessions she was full of idealization and basked in what she called "cupboard love" and a need for union. Sometimes the two ends of the club flipped unpredictably and alternated in wild succession. When she was in that state of complete identity with the polarized extremes—possessed by each one in turn—I used the image of the Dagda's club to steady myself so I could orient to the whole and remain relatively nondefensive.

Boundaries

The Dagda rolls his club along on wheels, and "its track was enough for the boundary ditch of a province . . . [which] is called 'The Track of the Dagda's Club' for that reason."[85] He pulls the club with its potentials for destruction and healing on the wheels of ever-turning process. The image suggests the balance of energies that are needed to mark human borders in the landscape of unlimited nature—to create order in the outer environment among disparate factions and in the psyche among divergent energies and desires. It suggests that such order is the result of a necessary compromise between destruction and creative renewal.

The Dagda's club is so heavy that it takes the effort of eight people to move it. This suggests that it is a godlike or Self task to hold the polarities necessary to create or discover boundaries in the psyche and to find order in the cosmos, to differentiate what belongs where, what is accurate, fitting and just. Jung reminds us that in several Gnostic systems the savior is called " 'the maker of bound-

---

[85] Gray, *Cath Maige Tuired,* p. 47.

ary lines,' the one that gives us a clear idea of where we begin and where we end."[86] Setting boundaries or making order in the psyche and interpersonally requires both aggressive separation and the holistic balance that we equate with healing.

Such boundary setting by the deity of abundance permits differentiation without destruction. Unlike the adversarial warrior's way, the king's boundary making allows all parts to coexist and express their own partial perspectives within the whole integrated structure. Like "fences that make good neighbors," the dikes marking each province facilitate security under the ruling power, so there can be both distinction and open and safe communication. The boundary making itself also requires the support of the wheels of life. These carry the weighty balance that represents the ruler's staff as authority over the opposites. The ordering process is thus alive, kinetic, not static and closed. Incorporating both assertive and inclusive functions, it moves and can change as part of the life process. But this method is slower than slashing away with a sword and is, thus, difficult for those who crave the adrenaline high of an emotional upsurge and/or cannot withstand the impulses to fight or flee, dominate or capitulate.

Boundary making in the psyche is necessary for creative life. To give an example: A client complained through several sessions about his sister's demandingness. He felt he had to listen to endless whining from the younger woman about their father's dismissiveness of her in spite of her frantic attempts to be closer to him. He met her daily litany with a silent explicative, but felt he had to endure hours of torture, although she heeded nothing he said. He felt she only wanted his collusion in blaming cruel, neglectful parents. When he was silent, she intimated that he should at least feel guilty, because he had managed to form a somewhat better relationship with the parents than she had.

Unable to get her to listen to suggestions or to stop her, he felt mounting resentment mixed with his empathy. He could not set an

---

[86] *Dream Analysis: Notes of the Seminar given in 1928-1930,* p. 13.

actual limit because he could not separate his own opposing reactions. He was initially even afraid to admit his rage and hatred, as if they were illegitimate and "wrong." Nonetheless, he felt mounting frustration and vented his silent curse to the telephone and his complaints to me. As I listened to his complaints through some part of every session, I recognized that I was being given an opportunity to feel as he did toward his sister.

I began to name the opposing needs he expressed about his sister, needs that I was also now experiencing with his litany. Both she and he needed to be heard and to be stopped or disciplined. As he saw how he had carried these needs in a merged tangle through life, the client's resentful giving moved toward both greater empathy and greater desire to set a fair limit. He saw that he had also needed both forms of parental attention. Accepting his own needs allowed him to clearly see his own inner battle between the two reactions. He stopped the whining to me that represented their mix.

Suffering sympathy and anger together but separately, he then struggled to find a life-affirming balance between them in regard to his sister. He rolled his way toward a compromise that made a fitting boundary based in the valid and polarized reactions. He decided in regal fashion that he could endure about ten minutes of his sister's complaining on the telephone. When he was with her, he found his limit was more flexible, depending on his attunement to the rising anger that signaled time for his cut-off. This eventually became a more reliable indicator of his boundary than an arbitrary time setting in advance. Nonetheless at the end of every conversation, he announced his limit, telling her that was as much of her preoccupation as he could take. Holding the valid opposites of empathic union and separation together in an ongoing process, he managed to make a living marker in the field of what became a more authentic relationship both inwardly and outwardly.

Such changing allotments of order are part of the Dagda's ruling function that we see several times in his mythology. This order is based in a sense of dynamic attunement with the demands of life, with what the whole situation requires in this place, with this person, at this time. For lack of a modern Western term, we call it being in *Tao*. In human terms it depends not just on ego control, but on the ego's attunement with the Self and the dynamic order that encompasses both conscious and unconscious needs, and personal, interpersonal and transpersonal relationships. Such attunement extends our potential for perspective and authority far beyond the warrior's more simplistic and adversarial capacity.[87]

The Wheel

One of the Dagda's names is Wheel. He carries his club on wheels, providing another image of balance. Here we see line and circle, assertive linear and containing round. The wheel itself suggests both completeness and motion. Through it we associate the Dagda with the round buildings he constructs, the round of the seasons which he calls through the year, and the vast wheel of the sun and stars he represents.

We also know the wheel as part of Ezekiel's vision of the godhead as chariot or *Merkabah*. We know it in the Buddhist Wheel of Life and the great flaming circle in which Shiva dances his creative and destructive cycles. Jungians often forget that their two-dimensional mandalas represent the whole process of the alchemical *opus* and a ruthlessly active *tremendum*. Sometimes, however, in our own dreams we may glimpse this archetypal image of the dynamic whole.

An analysand had a poignant experience of the Wheel when she was overcome by anguish because a contemporary event restimulated painful memories and raw, archetypal affects from her childhood. After confronting an authority figure, which she had experienced as arbitrary, self-serving and sadistic, she recalled her similar horror and rage at the unconsciousness and cruelty of Nazi authorities who had murdered her relatives. Her immediate family had avoided their own emotions with practicality defenses and a subtle

---

[87] Thus peacekeeping functions are hard for those trained only to battle, as U.S. forces learned in Bosnia.

blaming of the victims. She had felt that her parents had even identified with perfectionist Nazi standards in their behavior toward their children, especially toward her brother who was not intellectually superior enough for them. She lived with lonely rage at hypocrisy and strong survivor guilt that had made her a powerful advocate for the welfare families with whom she worked.

After a long struggle with her sense of grandiose responsibility for the personal failures she experienced from her parents as well as her own failure to accomplish a current, monumental collective task, she had a stark dream image. She saw a giant wheel propelled by sharp sticks that were hurled at it by an unseen force. These she associated to spears and bayonets. She noticed that some people were caught and ground under the wheel, and in the dream she wept. When she awoke, she was still crying.

Here an impersonal, destructive force pushes the wheel forward. In her associations, she recalled an earlier dream in which she was told she needed to put her shoulder to the wheel, and she also remembered the story of a child run over by a car. As we explored the emotional relevance of those images for her personal life, she also thought of her great-aunt once trying to teach her an old-fashioned, summer pastime—hoop rolling with a stick. We suddenly felt the deeper, celestial ramifications of that children's game, and she remembered the aunt as "a crusty, smart, no nonsense woman who spoke little and went her own way," and who years later surprised the family when they learned that she had been beaten and jailed for her participation in the Civil Rights Movement.

In her dream the wheel is heavy, and unlike the Dagda's, it does not carry the opposites. Aggressive energies make it move, rolling it over hapless humans. Struggling with the image, she was able to recognize the deeper horror she needed to admit: that "the slings and arrows of outrageous fortune," which she feared and hated as evil and tried desperately to control, might also be an impetus to move the life process along its way. And, as her aunt knew, that process involves pain and destruction as well as, and sometimes along with, creation. The recognition forced her out of a subtle and rebellious complicity with the defensive patterns in her nuclear family. Although she was the angry and scarred viewer, she could no longer deny the reality of a terrible fate by trying to claim responsibility for its operation through feelings of guilt and vengeance. She had to admit that she was only human.

The wheel represents an archetypal force. It is an aspect of the deity, thus beyond human or ego control. In this instance the dreamer was forced to witness its process. Slowly she began to move beyond her own debilitating, negative inflation, the secret omnipotence that she had carried in addition to horror and empathy. In this variation, the wheel image appeared before her ability to sense the opposing energies that it might carry. It helped her begin to differentiate her authentic reactions and human responsibility.

Through life we are faced with inner conflicts fueled by passions whose aims are as antagonistic to one another as destruction and healing are in the god's club. On a primal level, the opposition is represented by outgoing excited discharge that separates and destroys, and the inner desire to merge, incorporate and renew. Power against and need for are the ends of our primal club. They may become capacities for assertive individuality and intimate relatedness. In relations between the ego and the Self, they become part of the shifting interactions that Edward F. Edinger diagrams as a revolving circle, which he calls "the psychic life cycle" (opposite).[88] Our recognition of its circular processes provides psychological containment and ordering.

Ordering is itself archetypal. The ancient Irish saw it as a communal task or one that belonged to chief and druid. And inevitably we need help from others in our community or the individual Self or the godhead when we begin to labor at what the Dagda accomplishes so easily. The burden of holding the alternating polar emotions of separative aggression and mutual connectedness is too heavy for any one person alone. It takes eight people to carry the

---

[88] *Ego and Archetype: Individuation and the Religious Function of the Psyche*, p. 41.

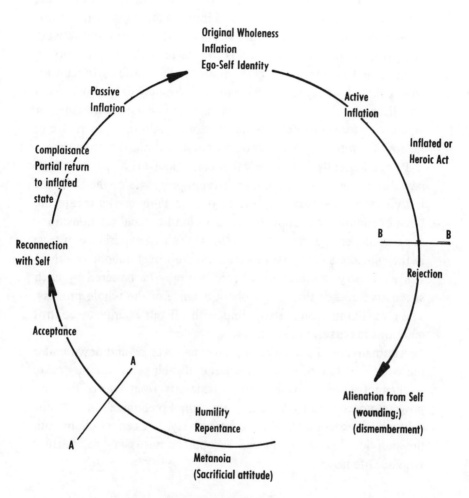

The Psychic Life Cycle.

club if the Dagda does not. The basic help required to bear the opposites is a function of parental support in infancy and intimate, accepting relationships to outer and inner others in later life. Contemporary research tells us that without early attuned and reliable companionship, our infant brains cannot develop the capacity to mediate and manage such raw emotions. Then affects remain archetypal, and we remain at their mercy. We may defend ourselves and dissociate from the complexed parts of our inner landscape, or we may be forced to stabilize our fear of the still raw experience of identifying with only one part of our emotional reactions at a time.

Psychologically, the wheels that carry the staff of death and renewal represent the ongoing, archetypal processes of the Self, our individualized wholeness. Within psyche their marks create the lived boundaries that allow both separation from and relationship to our complexes and their raw emotions. Without experience of trust in the caretakers who first represent the Self in childhood or others who can carry that archetypal role, we may be battered by each successive end of the club without a sense of the whole process. Then we bump along, struggling with all our energy to control emotions in ourselves and others.

Alternatively, like the dreamer, we may feel ground down under the wheels of fate or falsely in charge of their path. In either case, we cannot witness, manage, and disidentify from fear of the raw powers represented by the club. We cannot recognize our own coherence nor respond flexibly and creatively. We cannot claim both the individual sovereignty and acceptance necessary for dealing with our life issues.

6

Wholeness Through Incorporation:
The Vessel

Besides the club, the Dagda has an inexhaustible food vessel. It is one of the four treasured talismans of his people, the Tuatha de Danaan. "No company ever went away from it unsatisfied,"[89] or, in another translation, "ungrateful."[90] This bountiful cauldron—a vessel that we usually see as an attribute of the feminine—provides material and spiritual nourishment. Like one of his names, "Ample One," it suggests the Dagda's capacity to represent and engender abundance. Another of his names, *Daire* or "Fruitful One," was later carried by a Bronze Age ancestral figure, a chief who also owns a cauldron and a mighty bull.[91]

As the fertile, phallic partner of various goddesses, the Dagda epitomizes the potency required of all Irish rulers. Under a virile king, who also provides security and a just order for his people, the earth goddess is bountiful. The land's abundance is, in turn, reflected through the tribal chief's generosity. He provides good feasts for his people at their seasonal assemblies and for the poets at his nightly board. A ruler who is not generous could suffer the ritual of a shaming druid satire that would effectively end his reign. That the Dagda is connected to royal bounty shows up even in a late tale where he reappears as chief cook to Conaire the Great, a legendary Irish king.[92] The ancient god of plenty endures to ensure

---

[89] Gray, *Cath Maige Tuired*, p. 25.

[90] Rachel Bromwich, ed. and trans., *Trioedd Ynys Prydein: The Welsh Triads*, p. cxxxiv.

[91] *Daire*'s animal is a shape-shifter connected with druidry. Struggle for its ownership caused the Cattle Raid of Cuailnge, the events of which form the great epic of the Ulster cycle. See Thomas Kinsella, ed. and trans., *The Tain (Tain Bo Cuailnge)*, pp. 55ff

[92] G. Jobes, ed., *Dictionary of Mythology, Folklore and Symbols*, vol. 1, p. 406.

the abundance of the king's table.

As the principle of abundance and the ideal of generosity in an agricultural world, the Dagda is the male source of fecundity, the ever-flowing cornucopia in masculine terms. We can assume that the old bull god's bountiful and potent relationship with the earth goddess is representative of the degree of peacefulness known to exist in early Ireland. We know from archaeological evidence that competition for resources and struggles between the sparsely settled homestead groups seem to have been minimal until an extended period of agricultural disaster occurred. Tree ring research points to a time between 1159 and 1141 B.C. when there was an abrupt change. Throughout Europe little or no sunlight for eighteen consecutive years prevented summer growth and caused devastating crop failure and fear of the forces of nature.[93] The stress resulted in warlike activity to protect and seize scarce resources and an increasing movement of peoples around the continent. It also ushered in the Middle Bronze Age with the development of new styles of weaponry, ceremonial sacrifice to appease the gods, the building of defensible crannog settlements in Ireland, and the intertribal strife that marks much of later Irish culture.

There are similarities, albeit on different scales, between cultural and psychological dynamics. We recognize that one of the main causes of conflict in a family is the perceived sense that there is not enough time, attention or love to go around. Increasingly desperate neediness causes competitive struggles for the desired plenty that is seemingly withheld or given to a rival. Cain and Abel provide a picture of the outcome when the struggle erupts. When one party gains approval from a parental or idealized authority, the other may act out the destructive rage that deprivation can produce. The same dynamic may occur between generations.

A young man presented a clinical example. His cherished mentor had died one week before the birth of his son. He came into therapy

---

[93] Data from research on bog oaks by Irish dendrochronologist Michael Baillie. Personal communication.

at his wife's insistence, after he had verbally attacked her mother and become increasingly withdrawn. She accompanied him to the first session with the thought that they might need to be seen together. He spoke reluctantly and explained that his mother-in-law was interfering in his family. He wanted more time with his wife and thought the older woman was siphoning off her attention. He said he thought attention should go to the baby, but it was palpable that he felt sorely abandoned by a valued father figure and his partner. His wife was preoccupied with infant care, and while she appeared understanding of his recent loss, she made it clear that she missed her husband's involvement with her and with parenting their newborn. She admitted she was grateful that her mother was available to assist her. To the second session, the young father came alone and brought a dream:

> I am sitting in a kind of big sandpit holding [baby] Sam. I can't find any food for him. Then I remember, he's nursing and doesn't take bottles, and anyway I don't have one. Suddenly two hoodlums on motorcycles roar up and grab him and take him away. I wake very upset.

He associated the sandpit to a desert, "dry and desolate, nothing could grow there, a pit like in the movie *Woman in the Dunes.*" The riders with their black leather jackets reminded him of another film. In Jean Cocteau's version of the Greek myth, *Orpheus,* such motorcyclists serve Hades and carry Eurydice off to the underworld and death. Because Orpheus cannot trust that Eurydice is following him after he has won her return, he breaks Hades' requirement that he not turn to see her until the journey is over.

In this dreamer's desperate image there is no hint of the bounty of the Dagda. Instead the new father, who felt he had lost his mentor and his wife, had to face his sense of rote duty in the sandpit of life and what he experienced as his male helplessness in relation to the source. The dream suggests that he feels his newly born-to-consciousness, infant part cannot receive nurturance from a man, and the ineffectual father in him has no way to provide it. He lacks access to a nourishing source and has no mediating vessel from which to serve his basic inner needs. He feels abandoned by his wife, whom he also envies as the flowing breast. Like many new fathers when their partner is absorbed in the maternal role, he cannot trust the process of the beloved's return. He does not seem to know who he is without her. An eruptive force, serving powers of which he is unconscious, rides out to further disrupt the precarious father-son bond. The bond to what is new born is endangered inwardly as well as outwardly.

While little of this was understood in that session, the young man decided he needed to begin his own therapy. He took to the analytic process at first because dreams seemed so much like films to him and he was able to suffer their messages and work deeply with their images. His deceased mentor had been a journalist, who had shared his passion for movies. The young father had used them as a way to participate in the life drama while remaining safely distanced from his own needs and feelings. He quickly understood the concepts of displacement and projection. He came to see the riders in his first dream as an image for the lifelong abandonment and rage he had felt. He recognized that he was displacing blame for this sense of deprivation onto his wife's mother.

Inevitably the issue had deep roots. He came to see that the motorcyclists also represented the sad fate that had ended his relationship to his own father, a writer who had died from alcohol abuse when he was a child. With the threat of further fearful separation from son and wife, his dreams served to wake him up to a need to discover his own identity.

In a later series of dreams, he encountered male figures that were strong, abiding, and nourishing. One in particular had qualities that were reminiscent of the Dagda:

I am outside. It's a kind of grassy plain. I'm walking toward a man. He's like an old prospector, but weathered. Hard to tell, maybe he's not so old. He has on old Western clothes, cowhide, bent hat and chaps. The leather [is] gray with wear. He is singing, a mumbling humming, that does have words but I can't understand them. He is doing this singing as he stirs a big pot of oatmeal over an open fire. He's got an enormous stirring stick. . . . [He's] maybe like a ranch cook. There's more than enough in that pot for the whole crew.

This singing purveyor of what he admitted was his own child-hood comfort food became important in a series of active imaginations as an inner source of solace and guidance. Using the cook as an "imaginary friend" he could "sit around and talk to, and know there is always enough porridge," he began to find his own voice and to learn to express anger and need more clearly. In a later dream a similar figure showed him "how to love a woman and a man."

Over time, fathered from his dreams and in the analytic process, this lost son became a true father and formed a close bond with his own son. In the process he also joined a men's group run by an analyst whom the client had first encountered when he heard him playing in a chamber music concert.

Like the weathered ranch cook with his stirring stick and pot of porridge who knows how to love both genders, the mythological Dagda holds both club and cauldron. He symbolizes the energies of outgoing, arousing assertion and receptive holding and nurturance not yet separated into different figures. The Dagda's ladle also represents the containment and interchange of contrasting energies that are necessary to support a fertile life process. It is described as large enough to hold a mating couple. This robust *coniunctio* image suggests a pattern of wholeness that can both actively take in and serve out the abundance of life.

The Assimilation Rite

Not only does the Good God own receiving and pouring vessels, the Dagda also has a large containing body that represents an unbounded *yin* capacity. Called "Big-Bellied" and "Ample One," he is an orgiastic, gargantuan glutton, and he successfully accomplishes the ordeal of eating to which his enemies at the feast of Samain force him on pain of death. After he has single-handedly finished building a fort and its ramparts for them, and in order to prevent anyone from considering them stingy, they make him a porridge,

> for he was a great eater of porridge, [they fill the king's cauldron with] four score gallons of new milk and the same quantity of meal and fat into it. They put goats and sheep and swine into it, and boiled them all together with the porridge. Then they poured it into a hole in the ground, [as is still done today when food is offered to the spirits on Halloween] and [the enemy king] said to him that he would be killed unless he consumed it all; he should eat his fill so that he might not satirize the Fomoire [for being stingy].[94]

The Dagda gobbles it all, scoops porridge first in his huge ladle, then scrapes the giant pit with his finger, even eats the gravel and mold at the bottom, saying with gusto, "good food this." Then he fell asleep. His belly was as big as a house cauldron, and the Fomoirians laughed at it, for

> his appearance was unsightly: he had a cape to the hollow of his elbows, and a gray-brown tunic around him as far as the swelling of his rump. . . . His long penis was uncovered.[95]

The Celts were never fat. They took pride in a trim, warrior physique. Some of the derision here may be a later age's scorn of an older god—a "burlesquing [of] . . . ancient mythical ideas of copiousness and fertility associated with the [earthy] deity."[96] Nonetheless, to encompass reality, the Dagda here transgresses a cultural ideal—an ordeal we are often forced to undergo if we are to develop beyond our accommodation to social proprieties to become our individual selves. While we may not be derided in the same way as the Dagda in the process of individuation, we are often prevented by fear of shame from encompassing the fullness of our own reality.

Though wise, great, strong and good at everything, the Dagda is

---

[94] Gray, *Cath Maige Tuired*, p. 47.
[95] Ibid.
[96] O hOgain, *Myth, Legend and Romance*, p. 146.

here also a laughingstock, "a kind of monstrous giant."[97] But he does not feel shame at the mockery of his appearance. Corpulence does not detract from his primal function as lord of plenty, and he is secure in that ancient role. The eating ritual not only underlines the bull god's association with prosperity, it may have been part of kingship rites to prove the ruler's capacity to represent abundance. Magically and symbolically, if the god behind kingship can eat to engorgement, he can represent the cornucopia, the horn of plenty that pours forth bounty.

In a comparable ritual from ancient China, the king had to perform various tasks to prove his abilities and then "must prove it above all by filling himself as tight as a water skin."[98] We also know such physical engorgement on a body/ Self level as the symbolically concretized expression of expanded consciousness. It is similar to the initiatory inebriation with mead in the goddess Maeve's sovereignty rites.[99]

This porridge-swollen state of the Dagda indicates a ritual obesity not unlike that which was the prerogative only of brides in sparse North African economies. In a late Irish story, when the Dagda is in this round and expansive state, three rivers spring up before him.[100] Usually the mythic source of rivers is attributed to goddesses and to body fluids associated with the feminine. In the eating ceremony, however, the Dagda becomes a monstrous vessel of transgender completeness. As a male with a long exposed penis and swollen belly, he is positively hermaphroditic, similar to the grandiose Self when it symbolizes the *prima materia* in alchemical texts. Bloated from the eating ritual, the Dagda looks pregnant, and we might well wonder if there was some full-womb identification intended. Often in Celtic myth, pregnancy comes about through eating a small object, that is, through oral impregnation.

---

[97] Markale, *Celtic Civilization,* p. 263.
[98] Sjoestedt, *Gods and Heroes,* p. 55.
[99] See Perera, *Celtic Queen Maeve,* pp. 87ff.
[100] Gray, *Cath Maige Tuired,* p. 121.

The Evacuation Rite

In his hermaphroditic, distended state, the Dagda falls asleep and, when he wakes, is unable to have sex with a desirable goddess, the daughter of the Fomorian king, who fed him his overwhelming meal. We learn here that even the god can reach a limit that impedes the ongoing life process. He is not meant to stay bloated with what he incorporates. Unless he changes, he cannot do as the goddess requires. He cannot continue to function appropriately, so life wrestles with him as it does with all of us when we are in an unbalanced state.

> As he went along he saw a girl in front of him, a good looking young woman with an excellent figure, her hair in beautiful tresses. The Dagda desired her, but he was impotent on account of his belly. The girl [the goddess of the Fomorians] began to mock him, then she began wrestling with him. She hurled him so that he sank to the hollow of his rump in the ground. . . .
>
> He asked "What business do you have, girl, heaving me out of my right way?"
>
> "This business: to get you to carry me on your back to my father's house."
>
> She fell upon him again and beat him hard so that the furrow around him filled with the excrement from his belly.[101]

She literally beat the shit out of him, and we can remember that among his names are "Excrement" and "Great Decline (or Ebb)" as well as "Regeneration of the World." This earthy scene may have been a flagellation and compost-creating fertility rite. It confounds later Celtic and even modern categories of appropriate behavior. Although in contemporary biker culture, women may call their men "you shit" as a term of endearment, we associate such words with young children, who often take delight in labeling each other with the names of excrement.[102]

In general, we tend to think of the image of evacuation as related

---

[101] Ibid., pp. 47, 49.
[102] Susan Shaughnessy, personal communication.

to negative stuff and theories of the bad breast. It is not good food we throw out. To understand the Dagda's behavior, we can think of the baby not yet socialized to discriminate bad, stranger and shadow from good, family and ideal. At this stage the infant happily presents its feces as a gift to mother. Or we can think of the enlightened sage who no longer needs to categorize things in collective terms, because beyond distinctions of good, bad, clean, dirty, he or she recognizes the divinity manifest in all aspects of reality. With this image we can also see that recycling, which is a newly rediscovered archetype in modern urban culture, has very ancient, agricultural roots.

The process of incorporation and evacuation is one we also undergo psychologically. It is the opposite of sublimation. When we are too full of emotion to bear it without fearing we might burst or dissolve, we tend to pour out our feelings to another person or into some art form. When we cannot do this freely, our bodies often must do it for us.

One analysand of mine, trained to inhibit his emotional expression, revealed its intensity through somatic symptoms. One day he arrived at his session with stomach pains and painful burps. Having already been through several physical checkups without finding a physical cause for his discomfort, we knew that "something psychological" was bothering him. He said he had "already settled a difficult interaction with a colleague," but the practical outcome had not settled his stomach. It still burned as if he had an ulcer. He brought a dream:

> My neighbor is teaching me and my brother how to make wide-open pitchers for pouring cream or water. We use our hands to shape the clay.

His association to his brother was "timidity and politeness, or politeness and, therefore, timidity." The neighbor was "a sculptor who uses things like an old wire fence or wood from broken-down buildings to make wonderful animal sculptures." He can recycle pieces of fencing or building materials into new images of nature.

The man is, he said, "absolutely uninhibited. He can tell anybody off, but in a decent way, not explosively." The pottery process of the dream "is a bit dirty, but we aren't ready for a wheel, yet."

The uninhibited, creative inner teacher represents the dreamer's capacity to recycle the old limiting boundaries and broken-down structures of experience into more natural shapes. He is showing the dreamer and his polite timidity how to handcraft their own forms through which to express what needs to flow out—the wide open vessels that can hold and pour forth the contents of emotional life. While the dreamer and his timidity are being helped to create new vessels, he still sees the emotional contents polarized as "rich cream or plain water."

In another example, a woman who was struggling impatiently in a relationship she valued began to recognize that she could not find her own stance and style, because she was mired in reactions from her parental complexes. She realized she would like to imaginally create a pot—

> big enough to hold all the various parts of me that spew out and spatter us: the angry and needy and demanding and fearful parts. The pot could hold them, and I could sit and watch and maybe stir the bits until they stew into some coherent way to be myself, not just some wild, thrashing reactivity.

We can sometimes use other kinds of natural forms to hold what we are filled with and need to express. A woman in sudden grief found herself embracing a tree in the woods near her home. Dorothy Satten, a psychodrama teacher, recommends lying face down on the earth and breathing one's unbearable pain into "Mother Earth." This permits the comfort of "giving over" suffering that is beyond endurance into a larger context. Similarly, an actor client who could hardly bear the joy of her initial success made a ritual to give over its disorienting sense of omnipotence. She called it "the terrible, wonderful, intoxicating high. I need to give it back to the earth as fertilizer, because the earth can use it. And then I won't have to feel I will burst and die with the wild joy." For weeks after her performances, until she could grow a sense of identity large enough to bear the expansion, she imaged the excitement running through her and discharging into the earth.

The scene of the relationship of god to initiating goddess in systems theory would represent the process of an open, self-organizing system. After energy or information is taken in and used, some is let go or dissipated as part of the cycle of life and development. Here the Fomorian goddess is both the source of the energy/food taken in and the destabilizing force. She wants the man in spite of, or perhaps due to, his increase in girth (read complexity), which her tribe provided. So she continues the process and destabilizes him with her rowdy wrestling and beating. She forces him to let go of what is not useful on the new level, and she ensures that the excess, the excrement, be returned to the matrix to fertilize other forms of life. This is basic process in an open system on the agricultural level, on the living organism level.

As the text puts it more vividly:

> Then he moved out of the hole, after letting go the contents of his belly, and the girl had waited for that a long time. He got up then and took the girl on his back; and he put three stones in his belt. Each stone fell from it in turn—and it has been said that they were his testicles which fell from it [perhaps representative of his beyond-natural, tripled seeding of the earth goddess and again displaying his polar masculinity—phallic and testicular]. The girl jumped on him and struck him across his rump, and her curly pubic hair was revealed. Then the Dagda gained a mistress and they made love.[103]

"The mark remains," says the storyteller, "at Beltraw Strand where they came together,"[104] reminding the listener that the event had an impact on the landscape of earth as well as psyche. Like his tryst with the Morrigan that gave names to the ford on the Unshin River, this coupling also became part of the important Irish lore of

---

[103] Gray, *Cath Maige Tuired,* pp. 47ff. (reworked in Dames, *Mythic Ireland,* p. 106).

[104] Gray, *Cath Maige Tuired,* p. 49.

place names through which myth and land were interconnected to create a potent and numinous holding environment.

After their coupling, which is another earth-altering *coniunctio* of universal forces in human form, the goddess challenges the Dagda not to go into battle against her people, saying she will become a stone at the mouth of every ford he will cross and "a giant oak at every ford and in every pass." He replies he will then leave the mark of his heel on every stone and the mark of his ax in every oak forever. He asserts his equality not only in sexual partnership but also in magical and physical power. This provides another kind of necessary balance. As a commentator on Irish myth explains, the goddess of the old religion would "never tolerate self-abasement or self-contempt. . . . She wants a man conscious of his responsibilities, and worthy of her esteem and love."[105]

Satisfied by the Dagda's claim to equality, the Fomorian goddess agrees to aid him and promises to hinder her own people for his sake in the forthcoming battle by "practic[ing] the deadly art of the wand against them."[106] Unlike the young hero god Cuchullain, who rejects the goddess's invitation before battle and must, like all warriors, fight his wars with and against the mother of life and death, the Dagda reveres her, asserting the equality of his body and tool to win her collaboration in love and war.

The Dagda is an image of the full masculine, equal partner to the bountiful and terrible nature mother, because he is not split from his own "wholeness." Quite literally, he proves his fullness by incorporating the food of the enemy/other into his own person. He can voraciously take in, and he is also the repository of, enormous phallic power. Not only must he contain, he must also express vast capacity to fertilize by vomit, excrement and sperm, filling the furrow to support as many harvests and births as life requires.

---

[105] Markale, *Celtic Civilization,* p. 65.
[106] Gray, *Cath Maige Tuired,* pp. 49, 51.

Psychological Implications

We need to consider some of the psychological implications of the Dagda's eating ritual. We saw that the weaving of receptive and assertive capacities in the ancient Dagda is not gender based as it later became in Western culture. As Thor drinks the sea and Shiva swallows the draught of life's poison left over when *soma* was churned, the Dagda eats to engorgement. His is a divine capacity to ingest and metabolize the totality of life in order to meet and match and mate with the goddess. His image here suggests a possible way to live—not by repression but by expansion, taking in and metabolizing what is given to us to encounter, and letting go of what is beyond our present capacities.[107]

The negative shadow aspect of this gluttony is an unbalanced and voracious greed for more, for bigger, what today we call "affluenza." We see it in the appetite for drugs and oil and ever-larger cars and houses and other concrete things. It is a manifestation of our culture's deep insecurity and alienation from the ground of life, and it has disastrous consequences. We gorge and too often fear to give over, give back, give up, disgorge, and find our reverent balance, as the Dagda can.

Nonetheless, we can also see that the repressions of an archetypal appetite for life's fullness and ever-emergent process also helps to structure the heroic ego consciousness. The heroic ego ideal, with its emphasis on domination, must repudiate whatever is uncontrollable. It cannot tolerate change, which brings felt threats of chaos. We brand the discomfort and fear we associate with chaos as dangerous and negative. We push them away, so they fall out of our ego ideal into the shadow.

While this process is the price paid for a certain kind of binary consciousness and self-discipline, such aversion and superego imperatives required to maintain it, split off and repress instead of incorporating. As part of our repertoire, we need such discriminating

---

[107] It is very like repeatedly meeting and embracing the loathsome hag of Celtic sovereignty tales. See Perera, *Celtic Queen Maeve,* chap. 2.

consciousness. But if we can only process mentally from a separative perspective, we cannot encompass or accommodate the nonrational or learn to relate to otherness and the unconscious. We cannot thrive creatively to become the unique and multivalent individuals we are meant to be.

The Dagda's swollen state presents us with an extraordinary image—an appetite for life and a flexible, containing body/Self vessel that can accept and assimilate all it is given, even when force fed, and still say "good food this." Here the Dagda surrenders to the life process rather than willfully opposing any part of its overwhelming fullness. He does not order, discriminate or set rational boundaries against what is doled out. Instead he takes it in and waits for the inchoate, natural process of digestion to sort out what to incorporate and what to evacuate. He trusts an organic process. The Dagda's assimilation here represents a valid, deeply empathic means of processing emotional material. It images the radical openness needed for dealing with the presymbolic unknown. It models the humility that allows us to be truly open to the present. In T.S. Eliot's words:

> . . . the knowledge derived from experience
> . . . imposes a pattern, and falsifies,
> For the pattern is new in every moment
> And every moment is a new and shocking
> Valuation of all we have been. . . .
> . . . .
> In order to arrive at what you do not know
> You must go by a way which is the way of ignorance.[108]

The Dagda's incorporative way is slow and "ignorant," because discrimination of what belongs and can be integrated and what must be rejected operates through autonomous, digestive processes that work in darkness. This means of processing lies outside the capacity of our rational consciousness, yet we can develop some aware-

---

[108] "East Coker," in *Four Quartets.*

ness of it somatically and psychologically. We can taste a flavor or sniff an atmosphere. We can learn to sense that we are shifted out of a previous state, feel the influence of an emotion. In this intimately participatory, incorporative mode, we can experience the food as filling, expansive and life enhancing, but we can also find it sickening. Unfortunately, it is often inside us before we know its effects. Thus we face the possibility of ingesting material that is poisonous. We know a great deal clinically about the long-term negative effects of the incorporative mode as it operates between members in a family, group and even therapeutic relationship. Nonetheless, such intense attunement with the feeding other is a source of important awareness. "I feel her moods as if from within her," said one partner of her lover. "I can never get away from that demanding intimacy—as if he put his feelings into me to digest," said another.

Therapists are "fed" this kind of material when the client's primal emotions remain in a presymbolic state. In what is called the magical level of relating, communication is wordless and imageless. It occurs as intuitive or somatic perceptions. Jung uses the anthropological term *participation mystique* to describe this phenomenon.

On this level, the client's subsymbolic, emotional material enters the empathic analyst to be received, evaluated and hopefully somewhat metabolized before it is returned appropriately in image or words to fertilize the analytic process. As a colleague put this, "Sometimes [one] feels like a parent who has to chew an infant's food before spooning it into the toothless baby." At other times, when the analyst takes in what feels poisonous, she or he can be sure that a mutual complex has been constellated. On this primal level of consciousness, the analyst's work on the issue in her own psychology can have an equally wordless, fertilizing effect on the client in the therapeutic field.

Just as the Dagda needs the goddess's wrestling arms to allow him to splash forth the remnants of his meal, so we need some strong hold on our own life to remind us of our finite boundaries.

Then we can rouse ourselves from unconscious collaboration in the participatory communion to discriminate what part of the psychological material belongs to us and what must be evacuated. This process can occur when we wrestle to discover our own boundaries and the parameters of our personal psychology.

In childhood a client had been filled with what he described as his "critical mother's need for [his] emotional care." Defining this as love, he continued to feel nourished by how much he was needed. This allowed him also to maintain his precociously acquired sense of having "a large psychic size." Not surprisingly, he became a minister and a pastoral counselor. He entered therapy because a woman in his church had told him she would charge him with sexual harassment unless he sought help. He was amazed and felt misunderstood. He also brought a dream: "A woman, not my wife, is squeezing me to death."

He described his wife as "a fragile woman," repressed and critical. "She keeps me in line, but I am always disappointing to her." He said he loved his wife and had never been unfaithful, "although she does not care much for sex." The churchwoman was a new organist he "liked working with and loved as he did all his parishioners." In therapy he exhibited a childlike style of seeking the approval he felt he rarely got from his wife. After some months, he also began to exude the intense, polymorphous, erotic energy that his organist had felt. He remembered himself with his unhappy, doting mother, who had sat on his bed and fondled him until he went to college. The overcooked erotic food in his mother complex and the unmet childhood need for mirroring mixed with the unexpressed sexuality of his adult life. The indigestible jumble spewed into the therapy where he could begin to learn to let it fertilize a more potent, assertive sense of himself.

Like the Dagda, this man had been overfed and rendered passive until the exasperated feminine squeezed him, disrupting his identity with the ever-caring maternal role to which he was habituated. Like the Dagda's goddess, his inner partner, negatively projected onto his wife and positively experienced through the organist, wanted more of him, wanted him to assert his sense of phallic masculinity as her equal.[109]

I have come to feel that what we call psychopathologies have become prevalent today partly because we are more clinically astute in recognizing them, but also perhaps because we are meant to work more deeply to develop our capacity for integral consciousness[110]—a kind of fluid and/or transparency of awareness that permits using the potentials for multiple functioning that exist through our different structures of consciousness. Those who come into our consulting rooms inevitably bring with them problems embedded in primal forms of consciousness. In the areas of their complexes, they, and all of us, tend to function with magic structures or gaps between one structure and another. To work effectively with them, we have been forced to become familiar with diverse modes of consciousness to discover in which area the client is functioning, and how to communicate and find ways to help him enlarge and use his repertoire more flexibly.

For example, a new client suffering psychosomatic symptoms is communicating on a body level. A mental approach to her headaches will not adequately address their psychoid, emotional roots. Similarly, a defensively intellectualizing client cannot be expected immediately to express emotion or use imaginal forms through which to explore her psyche. However, the therapist, understanding the client's prevalent structure of wakeful presence, can meet and match it, and help the client to become aware of other possibilities. Thus in the process of doing therapeutic work, both therapists and clients develop toward an integral overview of the very ways we are conscious. We become familiar with a metaperspective in which "the various structures that constitute [us] must have become trans-

---

[109] As he worked his way through this material, he came to enjoy the psyche's pun.

[110] This term comes from Jean Gebser's wonderful volume on forms of consciousness, *The Ever-Present Origin*. His work was influenced by Jung's but is cultural and artistic, not clinical.

parent and conscious to [us]."[111] This is a radically new potential that is emerging in our age.

The current prevalence of character disorders may also have another cultural correlate. These disorders represent, among other things, attempts to circumvent the imbalances of the ideal, heroic, ascetically disciplined, rational, Western ego. I have begun to wonder if the pathologies are not a destined, though painful, means of personality development outside of, and ultimately beyond, the heroic paradigm. For the most part, we have tended to see them as disorders resulting from severe early deprivations and inadequate empathic relationships to caretakers at different stages of development. We say accurately, from this reductive perspective, that development is thwarted because there has been no safe and bountiful-enough place to incarnate appropriately. Thus early defensive styles continue to be rigidly repeated, as new information cannot be assimilated.

Some analysts in the British Jungian school, along with Winnicott and the British Middle Psychoanalytic School, see such pathologies as defenses of the Self that protect the emerging ego from unthinkable anxiety.[112] I think we can say that they have a prospective function as well. Perhaps like other symptoms that Jungians have always taken symbolically, we can also see the character pathologies as an expression of archetypal dynamics. In this context, they allow the pre-ego to maintain and/or regain connection with the Self, a wholeness not yet thought but still known as part of our

---

[111] As Gebser says, this integral or aperspectival structure is not acquired through an expansion of consciousness but rather through its "intensification" and a "leap" to a "fully completed and realized wholeness . . . [which involves] the reestablishment of the inviolate and pristine state of origin by incorporating the wealth of all subsequent achievement. . . . [It is] the integral attempt to reconstitute the 'magnitude' of man from his constitiuent aspects, so he can consciously integrate himself. . . [and develop a] faculty of consciousness [able] to adapt itself to the different degrees [or kinds] of consciousness of the various structures." *(The Ever-Present Origin,* pp. 97ff.)

[112] For a discussion of this perspective, see Donald Kalsched, *The Inner World of Trauma: Archetypal Defenses of the Personal Spirit.*

archetypal heritage. Created through the interaction of the individual's inborn style with potentials from the personal and transpersonal matrix, these early structures serve as false selves, identities that eke out what psychological nourishment they can and mitigate the fear and desolation experienced when the early environment is destructive. They also, however, serve to protect the individual's vestigial identity with the Self through the very forms of their defenses.

Indeed, much of the art of therapy lies in uncovering the styles of expression that replicate defensive patterns and distinguishing these styles from true Self-expression. Thus the therapist must appreciate how subtle are the distinctions between the authentic and the defensive and manipulative: how often love, assertion and need masquerade as idealization, rage and greed, or are altogether rejected out of fear.

Too often, both the demand for power, and the need and terror of domination, mix into our pathologies. As we work on them, we are forced to differentiate ourselves from the overly rational, competitive and simplistically judgmental style that our dominant culture prizes. As we can accept the aberrant forms that have sustained and will continue to shape our emergent individuality, we may find gratitude, softening and finally integration. We may—*Dei concedentibus*—find the internal spaciousness in which to metabolize the portions of chaotic life stuff we have each been served. Thus our distressing pathologies propel us to seek new, more abundant and profound ways of being and relating.

We can see attempts to right the imbalances of the heroic, ascetically disciplined, oppositional ego quite literally in certain kinds of obesity. Some clients gobble concrete food to compensate an overwhelming sense of deprivation or helplessness. They are driven to undertake the numinosity of size as if in unconscious identity with the Dagda—to become literally full enough of earthy porridge (of mother and/or Self stuff) to be able to survive their fear of severely imposed limits and the threat of abuse. Some kinds of obesity represent an attempt to grow a vessel large enough to contain what our destiny or the Self has presented us to deal with.

For example, a colleague dealing with Vietnam veterans found himself gaining weight as he sought to encompass the horrors of his clients' experiences. Until he began to work deeply on his own relationship to horror, he needed the food to soothe him and maintain his capacity to companion their memories and post-traumatic stress. After 9/11, I found that I was not alone among therapists unconsciously gobbling comfort foods to deal with both our own anxieties and the barrage of panic and grief of our clients.

Sometimes obesity results from trying to deal alone with the horrors of sexual abuse and other traumata. Then it may also provide the illusion of a guarding shield of flesh. More significantly it serves to create a concrete container for holding unbearable affects like terror and rage. Sometimes, too, in regressive stages of analysis, clients find themselves overeating to contain and assuage the primal emotions that have been stirred. They may get fat to balance the pressure of rage and need because they do not yet have a vessel of consciousness in which to metabolize archetypal energies and express them safely. At such a phase in one client's analysis, she finally noticed she was eating box after box of graham crackers. Only then was she ready to begin to address the emotional issues in therapy. Sometimes singers and psychics also become physically large to literally create a vessel that can hold the high vibrational energies of the Self as it expands into and through them.[113]

A client expressed her symbolic sense of obesity when she said:

> I told my lover that I am the nineteen-year-old he once knew, but also the forty-six-year-old married woman who respects the fact that we are both married now and have families and jobs we like. Suddenly I felt all the parts of me at once, smart little girl and all the ages and capacities of Me. It felt so large. I had a brief attack of self-disgust, thinking, "I am really fat. . . ." Then I saw that I am afraid to claim my largeness, to say "I Am Big." I think I am fat in body, but it is my identity.

---

[113] Joseph Ruff, personal commnication.

She behaved to herself as did her early caretakers, who had not accepted her legitimate early experience of omnipotence when she was still connected to her own wholeness. In early life she had to care for her foster mother, a deeply disturbed woman who had given her enemas to keep her thin. She remembered them as a "terrible pressure to blow me up." She struggled with a terror of expanding to claim her love of life and creativity.

> I want to write but I fear to go forth and swell, because I will be popped and emptied by someone's envy. . . . So I watch myself and who is near me to feel safe and small.

Over time she expanded her sense of identity to embrace the darker and passionate parts, what she called "the bitch and redneck." These could help her find new balance and grow beyond the easy, good child who had to be physically sick or hurt to get attention. She realized her completeness included rage, fear, exhaustion, forgetfulness, wild sensuousness, and the sensitivity that meant both joy and suffering could bring tears. No longer aiming for some old ideal of perfection as she moved toward claiming completeness, she often still had to discriminate physical from psychological size.

An overweight man, who had been on many diets, losing 40-80 pounds at a stretch and then regaining them, explained over several weeks:

> If I really took things in to offset the hungry ghosts in me, I would do a manic grab. I can't trust there's stuff for every day. . . . [There's] no sense of safe and slow. . . . Yes, I eat alone and a lot and fast. . . . Mostly, I guess, I try to get what I need from impossible sources that are just like the depriving ones of my childhood, which wanted me for their feeding and convenience. No wonder.

His food was not the "good food" that the Dagda scraped up with gusto. The manic grabs, like those of a bulimic or binge drinker, prevented his savoring anything he took in. At one point we decided to try a Gurdjieff exercise. Overcoming the skepticism and disdain that defended him from experiencing shame, he brought a sample of a favorite pasta sauce and cheese to his session. We each took a single spoonful, seeing, smelling and finally tasting it. We mouthed and chewed the textures, savoring them as we thought of each ingredient and of all the people who created the foods combined in the dish so he could feel gratitude toward them and toward the earth, air, water and sun that had made them grow.

Like the Dagda's appreciation of "Good food, this," he was claiming the food fully for the first time with another. Initially he felt a rush of fear and shame that he was a baby, no longer independent and tough. With the third slow mouthful, he relaxed and had a surprisingly joyful experience of conscious eating and communion. Quite appropriately he realized he did not want to manage the ritual alone, so when he found himself caught in what he called "blind eating," he twice brought more food to session. Otherwise, he learned to pause and imaginally return to the mutual sharing and his felt connection with the positive, elemental matrix he had experienced. Rather than heroically disciplining his addiction, he created a ritual to encompass his valid needs for life's bounty.[114]

Shadow as Source

In the account of the Dagda's bloating, we are told that his meal comes from the enemy camp. This suggests that the psychological material to be assimilated needs to be sought in devalued and spurned shadow places. Ego-identity will there be endangered, as it was for these clients, by being swollen beyond its own habitual and safe knowing of itself. The Dagda eats the chthonic "stuff," analogous to emotional *prima materia,* from the earth itself, unmediated by what is previously considered to be acceptably human. In us this stuff swells our hitherto shrunken sense of identity until we may feel fat and foolish and excited and emotional, and fear to spill out sloppily by raging or crying or babbling or peeing and shitting all over. This lack of containment feels monstrous, and we equate it with regression, a childish lack of control. It is certainly childlike

---

[114] See also Perera, *Celtic Queen Maeve,* pp. 386ff.

and passionate. It is also life affirming, for it holds the potential to grow us beyond shame into regal authority.

In therapy the image of Dagda's eating is often experienced as getting fat with entitlement, daring the bigness that is necessary to overcome the distortions of repressive development to claim the spaciousness of identity that we are meant to incarnate. It is very important not to label this as an inflation—a psychological term for the equally inappropriate scolding, "Too big for your britches." Such expansion does not represent an illusory inflation, for it is a regality rite and developmentally necessary. Nor is it like the terrifying perceptual aberration of certain schizophrenics, who lack an inner sense of body-ego and sometimes perceive their body boundaries as expanding to fill an entire room.[115] Instead the image of the Dagda can serve as a transpersonal mirror to show us that it is acceptable to be big enough, to swell up without shame. He provides a model for claiming what we have to metabolize from the latent stores of our potential.[116] Those stores are the source of a good ruler's generosity that allows us to submit, from a sense of plenty, to the goddess's embrace and readily release what no longer serves us but may fertilize other processes.

This confident claim forms the basis of authentic, voluntary simplicity and altruism. Such authenticity serves the life process, not a righteous ideal with which we might swell our identity in order to feel superior to others who are still wasting the resources of our planet. When I was an adolescent, my personal experience of the hypocrisy in this kind of righteousness felt particularly painful. Rebelliously, I reacted against it. Not surprisingly, however, the hidden judgmentalism in my own personality was projected. It en-

---

[115] This distortion makes the patient feel that anyone entering the room has entered the patient's personal envelope. The symptom implies a profound lack of the experience of human holding necessary to establish resilient body-ego boundaries. See Edward T. Hall. *The Dance of Life: The Other Dimension of Time*, p. 182.

[116] He is very different from the ascetic Shiva, whose attention Parvati—patroness of anorexics—gained by starvation and asceticism, and whose turning blue with the world's poison became a sign of divinity.

meshed me in relationship tangles with those seeming enemies, until eventually I could confess my disdain with a person willing to cook and stir the issue through with me. Then, from what had been an enemy camp, came some good stuff for me swallow. I began to metabolize the complex.

At first, however, I became swollen with a negative assessment. I tried to assimilate the whole problem and felt overly guilty. As we wrestled with the impasse, I could release that excess responsibility. As in the Dagda story where he had the help of the earth goddess to heave forth the excess, I began to deal with the material as something larger than what was mine to assimilate personally. It became fertilizer. My conscious understanding of the many entangled aspects of the problem of righteousness began to enrich my relationships. It also fertilized my book about scapegoating. In similar ways, the painful process of converting shadow material into ever-renewable energy continues through life. It can add psychological compost to the soil of each new season's crops. It can release us from the heaviness of our unassimilated complexes to walk with the Dagda as he bears the goddess of the life process on his great back.

Inevitably in the process of this claiming, the vessel of a companion, group or therapy relationship becomes an analog to the Dagda's big belly, his transpersonal capacity to hold it all. In actual therapy groups, the leader is usually given the role of the Dagda. Then like an embracing parent in a family or an encompassing, just ruler in a society, the leader strives to hold all the psychic material—even the pebbles and dirt—so members can feel a safe-enough containment to express and assimilate potent emotional material. As the group members develop trust in the leader, themselves and each other, the container role shifts to the collective membership. Over time, members of the group feel held as they experience and expose their shadow and projections. Issues of envy, competitive striving, shame, need, rage, fear, or whatever comes up, can be recycled to work through their complexed sources and discover the energy and meanings they hold. Experiencing a sense of the bountiful-enough and accepting matrix in the group enables relatedness, generosity and creativity in and between its members.

Diminishment—The Gold Coins

On the other side of the incorporative tendency to build a large enough body-ego vessel, there is asceticism—the need to control input by avoiding, measuring or purging, as if the individual is identified with the wrestling goddess and wants only effective, *yin* energy. Such individuals may repudiate their own access to receptive, incorporative potentials and try to survive "satisfied with crumbs" and spiting their own life-fullness. In identification with the ideals and controls of a phallic, heroic superego, they fear going beyond what is considered their adolescent norm, what one client called "my Barbie doll image of perfection." Thus they purge away every unconscious claim to be bigger, feeling it is too gross and an endangerment of the ideal that represents their bond to the collective, antilibidinous superego. This animus is a poor surrogate for the deity of life and death. Nonetheless, it functions to hide the client from painful process and the inevitable deaths that developmental change requires.

I think of a friend who had been terrified to let the passion of her considerable artistic creativity into her life. She feared for years that it would overwhelm the valued, safe structures of her domestic and work life. As a recovering alcoholic, she knew the surging compulsion that addiction brought, and she expected that her passion for her art might also sweep her away. She struggled with increasing self-diminishment to accommodate herself to the bland strictures of her daily round. When she became physically ill, she faced the impoverished state that her one-sidedness engendered. Then she realized she needed to find a more flexible and resilient relation to the conflict between her compulsion to create and her ideal of being the kind of good, working mother she felt she had never had. She saw these opposites as nothing but grandiose mania and dutiful, despairing depression.

The image of the Dagda represents a flexible body/Self potential to swell and diminish—like the penis itself. He can accept swollen and shrunken alternations as part of the masculine process of incarnated life. Although sometimes called "Regenerator of the World," he is also called "Great Decline." We have seen him bloated, yet at another time in the story he is close to starving.

When he is laboring to build King Bres's fortress, he is approached by "an idle blind man" who is one of the three satirists of his own tribe. This fellow has his mouth in his chest. Hence he is as voracious as a hungry heart, but unable to even taste his own portion. This satirist threatens to shame the Dagda's honor if he does not give away the three best parts of his food at every meal. Here, because the Dagda is the principle of abundance, and as a Celtic king must be generous as well as just to his people, he is susceptible to satire and shame if he fails to give generously. Such lack of generosity was what caused the poets to satirize Bres and drive him from his throne. Since the Dagda's identity includes the title "Great Decline," he can accept his own diminishment and feed the satirist, thus taking care of his honor according to the values of his tribe.

Since we must all follow social roles to some extent, we are susceptible to the part of us that nags on behalf of collective values. We can even view the satirist as a collective warning against self-idealization. When that part is deformed, however, as it is here, we might see it as representing an exorbitant desire to belong to the group. This needs confrontation if we are to become the individuals we are meant to be.

Initially the Dagda, kingly embodiment of tribal values, seems to be stumped and cannot deal with the problem of handing over the three best bits of his food except by acquiescence. He colludes in a way, however, that causes radical decline. He gets thin. Fortunately, and perhaps because he accepts his sense of diminishment and resulting need, he is open to learning. Thus when his valued adult son—a child representing a new metallurgic era—suggests a trick, he willingly cooperates. The son provides three gold coins to put into the food. Now giving away "the part of greatest value," the Dagda gives the bits of food with the metal in them. The satirist eats them and dies. When the gold is discovered as the cause of death, the Dagda is exonerated of crime in what is sometimes called the first judgment in Ireland.[117]

This story of the gold in the food suggests a trickster's way beyond self-starvation. It is a smart response when we are afraid of being shamed and envied, and yet cannot walk away from the shamer because he or she still holds authority. When we are dependent on the shamer as we once were on a parent figure, and as the Dagda is in the story, we then labor in fields that are not yet our own. The story suggests that we do not have to continue spiting our individual needs to save ourselves. If we are willing to oppose our identity with the ever-hungry, blind heart in ourselves, we can make a conscious sacrifice from the stores granted by our future development. To pay off what we still consider our debt, we can even use the coin of the realm, the standard of collective value to which we have access. But we need to carefully discriminate between such collective coins and our own individual feeling values. If we are too blind and hungry to discriminate, we remain beggars and are susceptible to having our authentic identity killed by those values.

To give you an example: an analysand with a father possessed by destructive envy had a terrible time claiming his creativity as a painter. When he began to paint and even to exhibit, he did so secretly, without telling his parents. The new work began to sell. Yet the artist was still shrunken in fear of his father's mocking satire and greed. He expected either overt competition or his father's repeated claim that anything his son did was merely the result of good fathering. Just after a show's opening, the client dreamt of a killer, who looked like his father, slashing a canvas. He realized that he feared his father, but more importantly that his inner father complex was still destroying his creative expression with contempt now directed at his own inability to feel confident and at what he called his "cowardly stinginess toward his parents."

After much anguish, he decided to do something that I think is

---

[117] Gray, *Cath Maige Tuired,* p. 31.

analogous to the Dagda's giving away his son's three gold coins. The painter told his actual father of his worldly success—the number and value of his works and their exhibits and sales. These were terms the father could understand and even praise, albeit to others. Afterward, the son said he felt "freer to breathe and expand fully." We can see that he gave coinage—an external value that represented his creativity in collective, concrete terms. This appeased the father's need for narcissistic gratification. The painter bought off the envious father by giving him the right to boast about his son's success. Each time the son's fears returned to erode his self-esteem, he had to remember the process of sacrificing the gold coins in order to guard his Self's true values and to keep his creative energy. It was a trick, but it was a trick that worked. And it helped the son to separate himself psychologically from his father and to honor himself and his own work.

On a simpler level, we may give an ingratiating, polite compliment to someone when we fear envy. In a variation on this trick, we play poor to flatter the other, hoping to deflect his or her envy and guard our own counsel and thoughts. Too often such a gambit becomes a habit, and we begin to identify with the diminished one. Then we may lose access to our own legitimate psychological size or hold it untested in secret magnitude.

On the other hand, when we fail to claim our own regal Self's authority, we are often in the position of the begging satirist. Because we live in an age of blind hunger too often divorced from authentic spiritual values, we are susceptible to gobbling up whatever another tells us are the best bits. We use our energy to envy, threaten and whine, failing to do our own work and make our own discriminations. We leave definitions of value to the one on whom we project authority, and we forget that we are seeking the source of bounty in one who is still a slave of outmoded mores, as the Dagda was in this tale. In contemporary life, this dynamic makes us susceptible to the brainwashing in collective advertising and political rhetoric. Unfortunately, while it may delude us into feeling that we are getting real food, it actually kills us.

7

Ordering Through Attunement

Known in stag, goat, ram, boar and bull forms, the Celtic Horned God is a cosmic figure, representing the kind of masculine authority that empathically rules over and protects animal nature. In myth the horned god initiates young men into adulthood and serves as guide between the worlds. He is the deity behind kingship. As god of the wisdom and druid orders, he mediates archaic and magic consciousness.

As herdsman and king, this figure suggests an ordering principle and the wisdom inherent in the vast instinctual world. In touch with his own animal being through embodied attunement, the chthonic nature god has the power to direct energy from within the ever-present flow of nature. He does not dominate arrogantly for his own aggrandizement. He tunes in to the flavor and need of the moment and rules in *Tao* with that. For example, after his servitude among the Fomorians when he builds the walls of their encampment, the Dagda is offered a wage. As the wise Master of Animals, he chooses a scrawny black heifer named "Ocean." And indeed when the young cow bleats, her sounds rouse the cow's maternal desire to attend, so the herd given previously in tribute to the Fomorians follows after her and the Dagda.

Such capacity for relatedness is very different from Cuchullain's need for domination. The heroic youth goes out to hunt animals with his stick and fierce, hypnotic eye. Then he ties them to his chariot and brings them back alive only because his masterful actions will be more impressive to the tribe's people and gain him more of their praise.

Humans need the capacities that both of these male figures represent. When they are combined in one figure, as they are in the Horned God, attuned relatedness shapes a particular kind of mas-

105

tery. We can see this in a Welsh tale in which the protagonist meets a giant herdsman who is Lord of the Animals. His description of the figure forms a close parallel to ones we have of the Dagda:

> A great black man, no smaller than two men of this world [is sitting on a mound in the middle of a field]. He has one foot and one eye in the middle of his forehead [a ritual single-focused pose found in Celtic magical and druidic figures], and he carries an iron spear which you can be certain would be a burden for any two men. Though ugly, he is not an unpleasant man. He is the keeper of the forest, and you will see a thousand wild animals grazing about him. Ask him where to go from the clearing; he will be cross with you, but nevertheless he will show you how to find what you seek.[118]

The man turns out to be even larger and the spear heavier than the adventuring hero had been told. The youth greeted him,

> but he replied uncivilly, so I asked him what power he held over the animals. "Little man, I will show you," he said, and he took his cudgel and struck a stag a great blow so that it roared; with that the wild animals came until they were like the stars in the sky, so that there was scarcely room for me to stand among the serpents and vipers and lions and animals of all sorts. He looked at them and ordered them to graze, and they bowed their heads and worshipped him as obedient men do to their lord. Then he said, "Well, little man, you see the power I hold over these animals."[119]

Here we see that the herdsman, through his horned familiar, deals with the animals by instructing them to do what they need to do. In the story, the herd's gratitude for his empathic attention gains the herdsman their obedience. Such cooperation is not the result of heroic domination but of mutual affinity, respect and need. It is the reward of the just Celtic ruler, the attuned parent and therapist, and our own empathic, integral consciousness. Experiencing the powers necessary to create such cooperative order is part of the Celtic ruler's initiation myth. It can also be part of our reclaiming the full-

---

[118] Jeffrey Gantz. tr. and ed., *The Mabinogion,* p. 196.
[119] Ibid., p. 197.

ness to relate to our depths and to others. We are herd animals. We like to cooperate as much as we sometimes hate it and need to go our individual way.

We can see the shadow side of this attunement when an individual uses such shamanic potential for personal aggrandizement. This can happen politically when a skillful practitioner manipulates votes by appealing to the herd instinct or hides self-serving changes in policy by stirring up fears of an outer enemy. It can happen in a session when the therapist, out of her own power complex, plays to the client's need for attention, intimacy, wisdom or protection. Often then a subtle high warns the therapist of inflation, or a dream of the client or of the therapist presents images that point to the illicit enmeshment.

The old tales can tell us something about dealing with potent energies that are represented here by the animals. They are amenable to focus and guidance if they are cared for and nourished. The herdsman god, like a good-enough parent, does not let the animals remain passive nor stampede; emotions and passions are neither ignored nor allowed to sweep through to destruction. When applied to our own relationship to drive energy, we can see that the motivation is based on perceptively seeking what is needed here and now—for example by consulting, tuning in, asking what the body/Self needs—and then following that primary, preverbal, holistic understanding. Such regal mutuality does not impose tyrannical control. Nor does it grab power by arousing a blind stampede or indulging momentary impulse.

Here the Dagda's model of authority teaches us how to perceive the whole moment with all its requirements, and then to cooperate with drive energy in order to shape it toward appropriate, mutually validated goals. The Dagda uses primordial, embodied empathy to guide with a motivation that the herd understands. Not an abuser or rapist, not a repressor, he calls the animals to follow his human form by respecting and integrating both the form and aims of the drive energy and the needs of his human community.

A woman with experience of an absent father and early sexual trauma had a transformative dream introducing her to this kind of male:

> A big man with his hair in three points walks into the room while I am taking a bath. I am terrified of attack, but he notices my fear and stops and hands me a big soft towel, and then introduces himself and starts talking to me as if he knows me.

The three points in the figure's hair made me think of Gallic, divine, three-horned bull figures and the triadic nature of much of Celtic material. Some other bulls and cows in Celtic iconography are portrayed as having horns that terminate in knobs. The scholar Anne Ross suggests that this may represent the nonnatural beast.[120] Given the context of this dream, however, it also seems to point to a partial inhibition of phallic aggressive energy in relationship that is an aspect of the horned god. In a druid ritual, the horns of the sacred bull are wrapped. Later Irish tales speak of bulls that give milk or are hornless.[121] This seems to be due to the equal balance of power between male and female, assertive and receptive energies, in ancient Celtic mythology.

Psychologically such a transgender sensing and ordering force comes through the body to both guide and be guided by the energies of nature. When discipline and energy are harmonized, we can experience this intently focused holistic order in the body/Self's capacity to flow in peak moments—in sports and battle, for example, or in singing, lovemaking or childbirth. On a more subtle level, it also allows us to attune to events and energy patterns in an individual or group and also within the nonhuman realm. The dowser's capacity to find water and the hunter's sense of the movement of game both depend on such broad perceptions. The order operates within the encompassing archetypal information field in which participants are joined. It is the basis of formal and final causality, what Jung calls synchronicity. It relies on a subtle, embodied inter-

---

[120] Ross, *Pagan Celtic Britain,* p. 304.
[121] Ibid., p. 307.

nal resonance in us, which functions accurately when we are open to nonverbal information coming from the matrix (which includes temporal, spatial, material and psychic events).

In this matrix, our consciousness and the focus of our perceptions are interrelated. The Zen archery master who shoots into the darkness and hits the target and then with a second shot splinters the first, explains that the goal "called" the arrow.[122] Such full participation in a unified field calls upon intuitive, proprioceptive and emotional sensors that have been sadly neglected as we developed mental and even mythological levels of consciousness. It does not depend on the separation of different forms. Rather perceptions from the inner and outer realm lie together and stir awareness through empathy, harmonic attunement, feeling with and into other via a capacity to let go of strong boundaries in order to sense parallel processes and similarities of form.

From an assertive *yang* perspective, this mode of mutuality consciousness involves entering fully into an experience. From a receptive *yin* perspective, it involves allowing oneself to be penetrated, to receive and metabolize perceptions and emotions in order to be affected within by their potency, a willingness even to be temporarily bloated like the Dagda, or poisoned as Shiva was when he drank from the spiral churnings of the cosmic ocean. Both *yang* and *yin* aspects depend on visceral and intuitive affinity. Scientists have only recently discovered neural cells in our intestines. Most of us have long known that sometimes we "think with our guts." Our ancestors relied on such modes of perception and saw the seat of sympathetic consciousness in the body.[123] Unlike our more detached modes, in this kind of consciousness the perceiver does not initially stand apart to discriminate between self and other. Instead

---

[122] Eugen Herrigel, *Zen in the Art of Archery*, pp. 66f.

[123] This was sometimes expressed in language. Thus the Greek word *splanchna* means bowels and figuratively, the affections and compassion. *Splanchnizomai* means to feel compassion, to have pity on, and *splanchnon* means both inward parts, entrails and the seat of the emotions. (Dorothy Reichardt, personal communication, February 2002)

the observer accepts that she or he is a participatory, interdependent part of an embracing psychic and physical field.

We associate such phenomena with primal levels of being—levels Jung calls psychoid—to suggest that matter and spirit are still conjoined. We associate these structures with projective identifications and inductions of emotional energy between people in therapy and other close relationships. Since this multi-sensorial perception operates through sympathetic attunements between body and environment, it can provide an often-accurate gauge of atmospheres, emotional qualities and complexes that have resonance for us in the repertoire of our own being. Although such attunement enables deep empathy, the attuned perceiver can also be overly affected by the psychic field, losing the capacity to sort information, to discern problems accurately and to see what belongs to whom. When that happens, projective identifications cannot be monitored in either direction—from client to therapist and therapist to client. In contrast, we can remember that the Dagda's club has two ends, one smooth, one rough—one giving life and joining together, the other confrontational and boundary guarding.

We have probably all experienced the "knowing" that rises as we think a name when we hear the phone ring or that makes us open a book seemingly at random and glance at a paragraph that turns out to be exactly what our next client talks about. Rupert Sheldrake is investigating these synchronicities experimentally with both animals and humans.[124]

Mediating passion with empathy, the Horned God initiates the young of the tribe into disciplined cooperation with the unified, sacred, chthonic order. We can see this as suggesting a means of relating to wild passion through initiatory rituals that allow, focus, and contain the energies. Just as the person initiated into the horned god cult does not remain in identity with his or her passions, so we may learn to manage our own raw emotions through the initiating rites and enactments of therapy. These include attunement to and

---

[124] See *Dogs That Know When Their Owners Are Coming Home.*

mediation of the primary affects and images aroused in the thera-peutic field.

The Dagda's Harp

The Dagda also relates to and shapes energy through music. Even in bull form, the god was credited with

> the magical virtue . . . [of] lowing every evening as he returned to his shed and byre. It was music enough and delight enough for a man in the north and the south, in the east and in the west and in the middle of the cantrel.[125]

Elsewhere we are told that "His very lowing puts all the cows in calf."[126] And we recall that the great harps of ancient Sumer had bull heads sculpted on them.

In a story from County Munster, we hear that the Dagda "comes from the *sidh* to harp the seasons into being. His finger breezes play across the gully strings where falling waters contribute to the mel-ody."[127] Here we see him as a masterful musician creating the vi-bratory patterns that shape the natural world. For the ancient Irish realized, as did the Vedic and Egyptian sages, that sound creates order and form, that "music is an echo of the original impulse of divine creation."[128]

They also knew that music changes consciousness, and many spiritual practices involve attunement to increasingly subtle vibra-tions through the use of rhythm and tone. The Sufi teacher and mu-sician H.I. Khan tells us that we develop spiritually through the ef-

---

[125] Ross, *Pagan Celtic Britain*, p. 166.

[126] Ibid., p. 167.

[127] Dames, *Mythic Ireland*, p. 114. The Roman writer Ammianus Marcellinus speaks of the Gallic bards playing the lyre. See John Koch and John Carey, eds., *The Celtic Heroic Age: Literary Sources for Ancient Celtic Europe and Early Ire-land and Wales*, p. 25.

[128] R.J. Stewart, *Music and the Elemental Psyche*, p. 45. Scientists now can con-firm that "the early universe rang like a bell." With scientific instruments, they are tuning into relic vibrations of the big Bang—"primal sounds generated by the cosmic microwave background that left their imprint on the matter-bound pho-tons." (R. Cowen, "Sounds of the Universe Confirm the Big Bang," p. 261)

fects of sound, resonating with subtle vibrations from thunder, the sea roar, jingling bells, running water, buzzing bees, twittering sparrows, the vina, flute and shanka, until finally we can harmonize with the most sacred of sounds, the mystical name of the Supreme Being. He calls it "the only name of the nameless which all nature constantly proclaims."[129]

Most religions use sound, rhythm and movement to shape and intensify the natural curve of emotional energy. Shamans and occult workers know it can build to the crescendo moment that allows body-mind consciousness to peak and reach altered states, even to be directed for distant healing. From body work and the ancient science of Mantra, we know that the vibrations created by singing and chanting affect the whole body, reaching to skeletal, visceral, neural and cellular levels. The Pythagoreans specifically advocated using music "as a medicine . . . as remedies against the passions of the soul."[130]

This ancient wisdom has been affirmed in current neurological studies. Modern science has instruments to study the effects of sound on matter.[131] It is also widely accepted by physiologists and healers that musical resonance affects health, disease and emotion. Scientists are able to show that sounds have a transformative effect on human physiology, to affirm that music vibrates the body at cellular levels. With brain-scanning techniques, we can even see that music alters consciousness. We can observe that processing music engages many areas of the brain beyond the auditory cortices that process pitch, melody, harmony and timbre. We can study how different rhythms trigger different areas: metrical ones (1-2) trigger left frontal and parietal cortices, and the right cerebellum. Nonmetrical ones (1-2-5, etc.) use more of the brain, both parietal cortices

---

[129] "Abstract Sound," p. 11.

[130] Iamblichus, "The Life of Pythagoras," in Kenneth Sylvan Guthrie, ed. and trans., *The Pythagorean Sourcebook and Library*, p. 84.

[131] Hans Jenny's work shows visually how different tones vibrate sand on a metal plate into specific forms. See Jeff Volk, ed., *Of Sound Mind and Body: Music and Vibrational Healing* (video).

and both sides of the cerebellum and the frontal cortex shifting toward the right hemisphere. We can affirm ancient knowledge with science to show that music arouses emotions and motor activity, which in turn stimulate more areas of the brain. We can study how all the operations involved in hearing and performing music can generalize to other aspects of cognition and improve mental performance. Those recently tested involve memory and the capacity to abstract.[132] We can hope that other emotional and intuitive capacities can be similarly studied.

The ancients were right that music is an archetypal ordering principle connecting us to the wholeness of ourselves in the vast, sounding universe. As a modern student of Hermetic music states:

> Originative music . . . is physical and metaphysical, biological and psychological, material and spiritual. It is rooted in the unknown, yet utters forth its presence into the material world as sonic vibration. It also has the remarkable property of rearousing the unknown, the mysterious, within the consciousness of the listener.[133]

A contemporary composer puts it, "Musicians are instruments of god's music and tune into the . . . source."[134] Thus "the role of the musician is to create balance on earth, to unite heaven and earth . . . to provide entrainment to the body's natural ways of vibrating."[135]

The Dagda's harp, with its resonating strings, is called the "Oak of Two Meadows" and "True or Fitting Four-sided Music." It calls the seasons into being. An instrument of divine, cosmic order, the harp plays only for its owner. The god "had bound the melodies [into it] so that they did not sound until he summoned them."[136]. The harp even travels to him when he calls it off the wall in Bres's banqueting hall, killing nine men to return to his hands.[137] (So his

---

[132] See, for instance, Mark Tramo's work at Harvard Medical School, reported by Nell Lake, "Cortices in C Minor," pp. 16ff.

[133] Stewart, *Music,* p. 44.

[134] Volk, ed., *Of Sound Mind and Body.*

[135] National Public Radio, "Morning edition," October 15, 2001.

[136] Gray, *Cath Maige Tuired,* p. 71.

[137] Ibid., p. 113.

harp is also warlike, just as his club is also healing.)

Then when it was in his hands, the Dagda played for them

the three things by which a harper is known: sleep music, joyful music, and sorrowful music. He played sorrowful music for them so that their tearful women wept. He played joyful music for them so that their women and boys laughed. He played sleep music for them so that the hosts slept.[138]

The fourth kind of music, one not mentioned in the Christian scribe's written version, may have been the arousal strain, which would set its listeners to activity and was used in battle. Such arousal is suggested through the actions of the harp itself, and we are reminded that the Dagda himself was one of the four Tuatha gods "who stir up strife among mortals."[139]

In contemporary studies we have discriminated more than four archetypal emotions and musical forms; nonetheless, the Dagda's harp provides an image for the capacity to clearly differentiate emotions. In many ways humans are like the strings of the harp, strung in necessary tension between the opposites, to sound the tones of life's songs. Until we learn to express them, we tend to leave our affects either blurred or radically one-sided. Then they remain maladapted and out of tune, polymorphous, or archetypal and overwhelming, so we cannot experience our full range to find clear emotional orientation.

Sometimes we flee the slightest thrumming as the threat of a crescendo on raw nerves. Then we learn early to dissociate and deafen our attention. Sometimes grief, joy, anger, fear, excitement and shame, etc., are blended together or mixed with sleep to relieve us of their powerful individual impacts. We may even quell joy with fear of past or future loss. We may stifle excitement or fatigue with fear of shame. Sometimes, like a single open string, we lose access to the broad spectrum of the Dagda's instrument and plunk

---

[138] Ibid.
[139] Ibid., p. 121.

only one frantic note. Inevitably we are taught to cover with a polite persona the music of the affects that our society labels negative and often, thus, fail to play our full range.

We can wonder if the god's four-sided music connected the emotions he played with the four seasons, four elements and four directions. The quartets in the mythology suggest some connection between number, time, emotion and acoustics, creating a true and fitting cosmic harmonic system that was the basis of later Pythagorean theory. For thousands of years before Pythagoras,

> music provided a meaningful correspondence between number and tone in the readily observed and easily measured correlations between string lengths (on Hindu-Sumerian-Babylonian harps) and the tonal intervals of sound."[140]

Perhaps the name of the Dagda's harp expresses also the ancient Irish view that the intervals which produce music are the same as those that underlie the harmonic order of the soul and the cosmos. A variant and expansion of this ancient intuitive science is emerging in modern physics as String Theory. Today, physicists hypothesize vibrating strings of energy that resonate with each other to produce not just four but eleven dimensions of space-time. Their harmonic interaction knits the universe together. While this is hard to experience, we may catch glimmers of the possibilities through manifestations like synchronicity, the effects of energy fields on animate and inanimate entities, as well as mystical experiences of Oneness. We will touch again on this unified view of the music of the spheres when we discuss the Dagda's role as builder and magus.

Like his cauldron and club, the harp also represents an aspect of the Dagda's mastery. Through it, he attunes with the deep, numerical order of the universe to create the flow of the seasons. Through it, he also tunes us. Like Orpheus, he possesses the seemingly magical power to influence the emotions of his audience and even to move or quiet nonhuman life. His musicianship includes being

---

[140] Ernest G. McClain, *The Pythagorean Plato: Prelude to the Song Itself,* p. 3.

good at eliciting, expressing and shaping a wide range of moods, emotions and levels of consciousness. Rather than inhibiting some affects, as do our ideals of manhood and heroism, he strums what he considers relevant into intensity and order through his "True or Fitting Four-sided Music." The basic quaternity of the Dagda's harp suggests an early modal system perhaps analogous to that of the *ragas* of India. The *ragas* use specific rhythms and melodies to attune with the qualities of different times of the day and seasons in order to both express the environmental field and balance the listeners within it.

The explicit way that the Dagda uses his harp also provides an image for what we seek to do with the many forms of art in life and in therapy. We can discover what we are feeling as we sing or let our fingers touch the piano keys. In a dream, music and song give the dreamer a potent orientation to affect and its meaning. Just as Pythagoras is said to have calmed the murderous rage of a youth by shifting from Phrygian to spondaic song, so we can elicit and modify emotions, ideas and physical activities with music. Music functions as a holding environment to permit relaxation of defenses and increased openness to the emotions and energies of the Self and the cosmos. Thus, some pieces may be avoided when they stir painful memories too deeply—such as the music once shared with a partner who has died. Conversely, music may relieve anxiety and calm the journey through difficult psychological material.[141]

---

141 The following e-mail account from Juilliard freshman William Harvey is an example of this. It was titled "Music Heals: Juilliard Story." Shortly after 9/11, for hours he and fellow students played for the families of the missing and their grief counselors and the men of the 69th Army Division, who had been called to help dig at the disaster site.

"For two hours we sight-read quartets (with only three people!), and I don't think I will soon forget the grief counselor from the Connecticut State Police who listened the entire time, or the woman who listened only to 'Memory' from *Cats,* crying the whole time. . . .

"At 7, the other two players had to leave; they had been playing at the Armory since 1 and simply couldn't play any more. I volunteered to stay and play solo, since I had just got there. I soon realized that the evening had

It can reach even farther. An elderly singer with severe Alzheimer's disease can remember and sing operas, although she cannot name her children or say what day it is. She becomes radiant listening to music that evokes memories, while ideas, opinions and verbal knowledge have gone.[142]

A client who was fearful of "falling into the unconscious and going psychotic" cringed from relaxing the desperate defenses that warded off her own emotional depths along with painful memories of neglect and a fire in which she had been badly burned. After much therapy, she had a reorienting dream that allowed her to sense a deeper order that could hold her as she softened toward her overwhelming emotions:

> I am in Central Park where people are doing an important ritual. A woman explains that I am to play an instrument along with others. We talk about music and my love and experience with it. Then I am given my instrument and told where I will sit so I can see and follow the conductor. It is a difficult piece, but I have apparently already been auditioned.

---

just begun for me: a man in fatigues who introduced himself as Sergeant Major asked me if I'd mind playing for his soldiers as they came back from digging through the rubble at Ground Zero. Masseuses had volunteered to give his men massages, he said, and he didn't think anything would be more soothing than getting a massage and listening to violin music at the same time.

"So at 9:00 p.m., I headed up to the second floor as the first men were arriving. From then until 11:30 [p.m.], I played everything I could do from memory: Bach . . . Tchaikovsky [and] Dvorak [to opera and] . . . Theme[s from movies and folk songs] . . . . Never have I played for a more grateful audience. Somehow it didn't matter that by the end, my intonation was shot and I had no bow control. I would have lost any competition I was playing in, but it didn't matter. The men would come up the stairs in full gear, remove their helmets, look at me, and smile."

[142] Her son, commenting on National Public Radio, said, "Something essential is left, the sadness without content of her mother's leaving her when she was a child and a sense of direct, visceral, utterly present experience of music. ("The next Big Thing," Sunday, January 12, 2002) See also Jeff Volk's video, *Of Sound Mind and Body,* for other examples of the use of music with Alzheimer's patients, hospitalized patients with cancer, and with the dying.

Here she is to deal with a central issue in a ritually ordered way. The archetypal structure of music itself will be conducted and mediated to her through a Self figure. The dream tells her she has been through the preliminaries—"been auditioned"—and is ready for the challenge of a difficult piece of life's music.

Sometimes music therapists start with music that reflects the current emotional state of their patients to intensify it and encourage abreaction. The music shapes the emotional release so it is held more or less safely within the structure of the piece as well as by the empathic personal attention of the therapist.[143] Sometimes, in hospitals with chronic clients, therapists may start a session by matching the music with the patient's emotional state and then play a series of pieces that shift along a gradient to evoke other emotions. For example, with depressed patients they may start with slow, heavy music, then play pieces with different tones and rhythms to elicit increasingly more serene and upbeat responses. At other times therapists in clinics and classrooms use music that will bring about a desired emotional state. Thus Mozart may be used to help focus attention (as well as to stimulate milk production with cows and egg laying with hens). Researchers and clinicians at The Monroe Institute use specific vibrations matched with brain frequencies, often embedded in composed music, to directly effect neural activity and states of consciousness.[144]

Even when not working with music as therapy, I have found that there is much that is musical in the therapy work with emotional states and complexes. Every voice has many moods and a distinct personality. Like body language, it cannot be easily disguised. Thus the voice is filled with authentic psychological meaning. Every vocal nuance can mirror what is in the psyche—expressing much more than the words it speaks. The attentive listener finds in the nonverbal musicality of a voice the clues to hidden affect, issues of

---

[143] See Mary Marsh's study of her work as a music teacher with young children. (Unpublished manuscript for Ste. Anne's school, Brooklyn.)

[144] See the Monroe Institute website: www.monroeinstitute.org.

persona and shadow, qualities of inner and outer relatedness available at the moment. I try to listen for the colors and shifts of pitch and range, and the richness or constriction in tonal harmonics (the over- and undertones), rhythm, pace and breath. Silences too are filled with psychological information and meaning.

The voice, as our most readily available instrument, expresses the whole Self. Its resonance or constriction tells us about comfort or withholding in relation to the Self. For example, the voice's range, if narrowed into monotone, or artificially lowered or raised, may reflect persona issues, a need to act overly tough or timid, for example.[145] Nasality may clue the listener to unconscious or passive aggression. Whininess may suggest a struggle between the energy of release and holding back or between two other divergent impulses. Breathiness may reveal a discomfort with embodiment and/or an intense need to communicate a spiritual message. A held-back voice may suggest a learned incapacity for forthrightness or a need to get the listener to come emotionally toward the speaker. Pressured pace and tone may imply counterphobic assertiveness or a need to claim or deter attention.

When there are discrepancies between word, body language and voice, the listener is immediately given nonverbal symbolic, embodied experience of an active complex. We are made uncomfortable by that kind of double message, and therapists are trained to attend to its meanings. The many qualities conveyed in the voice alone are worth noting, for they deeply affect the possibilities of communication in the relationship between client and therapist and between the speaker and Self.

Decades ago, studying voice with Joseph Ruff, I became aware of how much can be gleaned about personality from even a few sentences on the phone. That is one of the ways I assess whether or not I will be a good fit for a prospective client. It also allows me to better follow and participate in the musical aspects of communica-

---

[145] See Martha Mae Newell, "Sounding Through the Mask: The Person and Sound," pp. 49ff.

tion during psychotherapy sessions. Studying Neurolinguistic Programming, I learned the value of listening to and even accompanying tonal pace and quality as well as breath patterns—what we might call vocal mirroring. This not only provides a sense of companionship for the client, it also helps the therapist to begin to attune adequately with a client's emotional state by direct experience of its internal effects. Sometimes, listening intently, we can discern hints of the client's voice before she or he learned language or developed the complexes that created the current emotional dynamics. And when the youngest part of the client is present, I sometimes find myself using the preverbal sounds that originate in the acoustic repertoire of mother and baby.

Inevitably, I pay a lot of hovering, barely conscious, nonverbal attention to the music in a session and read it (along with all the usual material) to attune with the preverbal, emotional harmonics within a client and in the field between that person and myself. I try to use that sense of harmonics to steer toward or away from crucial areas of intensity that need or resist attention. Some sessions seem filled with mutual participatory sound and content; they feel like the playing of improvisational duets. Other sessions feel more like explorations of a theme. Others bounce all over or nearly deafen my imagination with noise. Still others sink into silences so deep that I have to listen for the wisps of breath in my imagination to find clues to the emotional whereabouts of my client. Steven Knoblauch has recently written of this nonverbal exchange as the basis of the transformative aspect of dialogue. He names it "the musical edge of therapeutic dialogue." For me, it might equally be called the musical core.

I think that musical training, or training in any art or in art appreciation, is indispensable for all of us, and especially for therapists. It awakens the inner senses to track the themes and variations that play through every session, every interchange, every day, through the many dimensions of human experience. As we remember similarities and notice divergences, we learn to recognize the deep energy patterns underlying and creating all the surface elements. The deep vibratory structures resonate as mythic images and rites, as symbols. These archetypal patterns also express themselves in personal complexes, behaviors and relationships, in all the many forms of art, as well as in all the ways we live out personal and collective history. Through them all, we can hear the varying tensions of the harp strings and the fingers of the cosmic musician strumming time and the seasons, ourselves and our changing cultures into and out of existence.

8

Wholeness Through Alignment
with Earth and Cosmos

The Dagda's third partner is Boann, ancient goddess of the River Boyne and Newgrange. Her river, Latinized as Bouvinda, was still used as the name of Ireland in Ptolomy's second-century A.D. geography. The word *vind* (Irish *find*) means wisdom, inspired illumination or discovery, and was the name of several ancient Irish seers and also a class of druids. Bouvinda's waters would have been viewed not only as the source of life-giving force and fertility to the surrounding countryside, but also as "the mystical stream which was distributed through the seers."[146] Boann's name in Irish means white cow. She is a Great Mother goddess and the source of nourishing milk as well as celestial wisdom.

The goddess Boann's vast earth temple, the Brugh Na Boyne or Newgrange, sited in the curl of her river near two other large passage mounds, is older than the pyramids. There is a tradition that the Dagda himself built it.[147] Called by medieval scribes a "fairy mound," a "fairy mansion," and the "Bed of the Red Dagda," its architecture creates and expresses links between the patterns of earthly life and sky that were known to the ancient seers. Its inner initiatory incubation and burial chamber is aligned with the winter solstice sunrise. The same medieval place-name poem also describes the Brug as "a king's dwelling . . . a shelter, [and]. . . a keep renowned for strength.[148]

Its form is awesome: an immense earthen dome with an encircling band of intricately carved megaliths surmounted by glittering white quartz studded with smooth, gray river stones. Its inner

---

[146] O hOgain, *Myth, Legend and Romance*, pp. 208f.
[147] Gwynn, ed., *The Metrical Dindschenchas*, vol. 2, p. 19.
[148] Ibid.

structure is the setting for a wondrous yearly event. At the winter solstice sunrise, for twenty minutes the sun's rays pierce the long passage through a roof box over the lintel. The sunlight moves into the cruciform center of the mound and its three chapels to illuminate the carvings there. The myth of the Dagda and Boann replicates this archetypal happening. We are told that the Dagda finds the goddess in her great temple and makes love to her there while her husband is away.[149]

> He came [to the Brugh] by chance and fell to importuning Boann . . . .
> Boann said "Union with thee, that were my primary desire."[150]

So the Dagda enters the Brugh "to lie with the lady Boann,"[151] moving as rising sun into the center of her belly mound at the darkest time of the year. Then, with sorcery, the story tells us, "they made the sun stand still to the end of nine months."[152] The Dagda controls time and the seasons to make nine months seem like a single day, so that he and the ever-young goddess can enjoy themselves in timeless bliss and let her pregnancy come to fruition before her other partner returns.

This erotic paradise is very different from that of the Judeo-Christian Bible. More like the *Song of Songs*, the poetry of the goddess Inanna and the sacred erotic sculptures of India, the story of the Dagda and Boann celebrates the equality of female and male deities joined in ecstatic, fruitful lovemaking. The mythic tryst of the couple at the winter solstice birthed the new light. This third cosmic *coniunctio* in the Dagda's legend, along with evidence in many other Celtic stories, suggests again the very strong possibility of an ancient tradition of sacred sexual rites in early Ireland.

From myths and a traveler's eye-witness account, we know of sovereignty rites in which the chosen ruler engaged in sacred sexual intercourse with a woman or animal that represented the god-

---

[149] "The Wooing of Etain," in Gantz, *Ancient Irish,* p. 39.

[150] Gwynn, ed., *The Metrical Dindschenchas,* vol. 3, p. 37.

[151] O hOgain, *The Sacred Isle,* p.18.

[152] Gwynn, ed., *The Metrical Dindschenchas,* vol. 3, p. 37.

dess.[153] This act affirmed the chief's capacity and right to rule the goddess's land. The coupling of the Dagda and Boann suggests what may have been a longer erotic initiation inside the great temple mound to incubate enlightened, mystical consciousness. As we learn from numerous tales, some form of sexual ritual may well have helped the poets and predruidic magi acquire their inspiration and *gnosis*.[154] This powerful physical alchemy to alter consciousness has been a hidden mystery in the West because of the strong aversion to nature and the feminine in official, exoteric Judeo-Christian institutions. Ritual transformation of erotic energy into deep, spiritual bliss was practiced in Chinese and Indian yoga and in the Gnostic, alchemical and Western occult traditions deriving from Egypt. We can see another source of this spiritual practice in the Irish ritual that took place in Newgrange and probably many other goddess temples throughout the Neolithic world.

In the myths, *Aonghus* (meaning "real vigor"), the child who was born in the initiatory retort of the ancient temple mound, represents the beginning of a new age. He is associated with gold, perhaps hinting at the transmutation of consciousness in ancient alchemy. In myth, he is the smart lad who helps his father out with the trick of gold coins. Angus, called the "Mac Oc," the son of the ever-young couple, is also the foster father and rescuer of the heroes of the culture just birthing in Ireland with the age of metallurgy.

---

[153] See Perera, *Celtic Queen Maeve*, esp. chaps. 1 and 2.

[154] Gaelic motifs suggesting such an erotic form of gnosis occur in several tales: Bran's Voyage and sojourn on the Island of Women, Tom the Rhymer's journey with the Goddess to acquire poetic vision and truth, Diarmuid's journey with Grainne, Tristam/Tantris's devotion to Iseult, Tannhauser's connection to the Venusberg, Meilyr's gift of prophecy from his beloved's lap, among many others. (See Perera, *Celtic Queen Maeve*, p. 104) While some of these are disguised, others are obvious. The erotic rites in the Old Religion and the fierce convictions of witches for their lovemaking with the horned god point to the same dynamic. That the stories are known in versions contemporary with the Troubadour tradition does not obviate their older and deeper significance.

Magical and Druidic Functions

The Dagda's lovemaking with the Morrigan connects him with the chief's role in war and healing. His lovemaking with the Fomorian goddess represents his part in ancient fertility rites. This relationship with Boann calls our attention to the Dagda's function as a shape-shifting magus and master of what later became druidry. Here the horned bull god is mate of the cosmic cow goddess, who is herself mistress of the river of life and the celestial Milky Way.

An old riddle asks, "Who was king over all Erin, sweet-sounding, radiant?" Then it answers, "Who but the skillful Dagda."[155] Skillful, sweet-sounding and radiant he was. He is sometimes described as a "glowing head" and "one-eyed"—fitting names for the divine godhead filled with mystic vision. Both images connect him with the Stone Age solar lore manifest in the architecture of Newgrange.[156]

This "Lord of Perfect Knowledge" is also named "Lord of The Wisdom of the Oak," a tree we recognize as particularly sacred to the druid order. Roman writers describe oak groves in which the Celts worshipped and sacrificed. As a fitting world axis, the majestic, long-lived tree is known to attract bolts of lightning from the sky, while its roots reach deep into the earth and often enclose the wellspring of knowledge. Its branches provide shelter, and its mast of acorns provide nourishment. We are told that during the ceremonial cutting of sacred, healing mistletoe from the oak branches, the druids sacrificed two white bulls with their horns bound for the first time.[157] Bulls were also used in divination rites. A bull was sacrificed and a druid ate his fill of its broth and meat and slept in its skin in order to dream of the next king.

The Dagda, the bull god and "Lord of the Wisdom of the Oak," is himself named as "a god of druidry" and the "multiform tri-

---

[155] Gwynn, ed., *The Metrical Dindschenchas*, vol. 4, p. 105.

[156] O hOgain, *The Sacred Isle*, p. 60, note 10. At a later time he was also connected with the Bronze Age solar cult.

[157] Pliny, quoted in Koch and Carey, eds., *The Celtic Heroic Age*, p. 26.

ads."[158] One of his names is "Triad." These triads are a form of memory device in which "the perfection of the [druid] . . . science" is codified. Roman writers tell us the druids were "an intimate fellowship," comparable to the Magi of the Persians and the Brahmins of India.[159] They followed "the doctrine of Pythagoras. . . seeking the unseen, making little of human mortality as they believed in the immortality of the soul."[160] "They claim to know the size of the earth and cosmos, the movements of the heavens and stars, and the will of the gods."[161]

The Dagda is master of all the arts that made up druid lore—the technical and magical control of natural forces, music, poetic incantation, healing and prophecy. Ruling from Newgrange, the great Neolithic temple complex, he is also a cosmologist and master of the astronomy that was manifest in the architecture of Old Europe and ruled the activities of the ancient world. We have seen that he was intimately connected with time in all its interrelating cycles—cosmic, agricultural and animal—including the body-time of pregnancy. He had the wisdom and force to rule time, by stopping the seasons to let his son be born, by harping them around the year.

The curious second name of the harp, translated "True" or "Fitting, Four-sided, Rectangular, or Square Music," suggests an aspect of the Dagda that has hitherto been overlooked. This aspect is connected to proto-Pythagorean theories of number, harmonics, astronomy and geometry. We know that the Dagda is also a builder. Maker, musician, cosmologist, life-giver and builder, he is the Irish creator god, working with mind and hands to erect great, circular, religious and royal structures across the ages.

He is the traditional builder of New Grange, the fourth millen-

---

[158] O hOgian cites a reference that states that the Tuatha De Danaan, "themselves had a god of druidry, Eochaidh Ollathair (Horseman, Father of all), the great Daghdha." (*The Sacred Isle,* p. 61)

[159] Dion Chrysostom, quoted in Koch and Carey, eds., *The Celtic Heroic Age,* p. 24.

[160] Ammianus Marcellinus, quoted in ibid., p. 25.

[161] Pomponius Mela, ibid., p. 25.

nium temple so wondrously aligned with astronomical events and the cosmic "Wheel" that, you remember, is one of the Dagda's names. Here his practical creative work links human architecture to those cosmic cycles. He also erected Bres's fortress and the earthworks around it. And he is credited with ordering the building of a much later, remarkable circular fort on a sacred hilltop at Ailech in Donegal—a site near the central northernmost tip of Ireland. Traditionally this is said to have been his own home, because it is the "hill where the Dagda slept."[162] Alternatively, it is called the burial place for his son, because it is the "Hill of Tears for the Dagda's tears in mourning for his son, Aed."[163] The massive stone cashel stands in the center of the horizon circle near a holy well now sacred to St. Patrick. Its only door faces due east toward the rising sun. The Bronze Age structure lies inside three much earlier Neolithic earth rings on a height where once an ancient megalith stood.[164] Legend tells us that this Grianan (sun house) was

> built of red yew tooled and arched overlaid with pure unwrought silver and gold and bronze. It was decked inside with bright gems . . . [so that] alike were day and night in the midst of it.[165]

---

[162] Gwynn, *The Metrical Dindschenchas*, vol. 4, p. 107.

[163] Ibid., p. 237.

[164] Rather than destroying the murderer of his son, the Dagda ordered him to bring a "stone that shall be a trophy over Aed's grave." The fellow found such a megalith "over Loch Foyle and raised it up with a champion's strength . . .[and] bore the burden over road after road . . . until his heart burst in the height of Ailech." (Ibid., p. 103)

[165] Ibid., p. 107. The Grianan was built in 1700 B.C. according to the Visitor's Centre brochure. In it St. Patrick baptized Owen, prince of Inis Eoghain. In the fifth century A.D., the Ui Neills, overlords of Ulster and High Kings of Ireland, made it their royal residence. Its name is glossed as *ailech*, which means rock, foundation, satire, dung heap, or stone building of a sunny place, stone house with a view, and stone house of the sun. Tradition tells us that the old Tuatha god, Nuadu, was buried here, and that Ailech was a Scottish princess. The flight of the earls was from nearby Loch Swilly at Rathmullan, and sleeping warriors are said to lie in a cave near the Grianan waiting to awaken with a new leader. The wellspring between two outer banks on South side, now called *Tober Phadraig*, is connected with a Neolithic tumulus and Late Bronze Age remains.

Michael Dames suggests that

the Grianan thus stood for a state of equilibrium prior to seasonal
and diurnal fluctuation . . . an equivalent to the Indian condition of
atman, where the undifferentiated world soul is revealed at the deepest level of individual awareness.[166]

Like Newgrange, the wheeling stars, the horizon, and the god himself, this round structure also expresses totality.

The Dagda is the only Irish deity I can think of who constructs
with his own hands. Other Celtic figures carry wood or cut trees or
hunt but do not create structures of earth and stone. His building
capacity and his true, fitting, four-sided harp and music suggest that
he embodies and enacts the wisdom of the pan-European, proto-
Pythagorean cult that was concerned with cosmology, "with the
heavenly bodies, their meanings and magic and their influence on
our world."[167] Based in an awareness we can barely comprehend,
its masters created the marvels of Stone Age architecture in Anatolia, the temple-tombs on Malta, Old Europe, and the pyramids of
Egypt. We can appreciate their sacred geometry as we study the
shapes and alignments of structures throughout the megalithic
world. Some scholars now recognize that their units of measure-
ment—the megalithic yard and rod—are related to the diameter of
the earth.[168]

Their stonemasons created carvings that have awesome beauty
and hieroglyphic mystery. These stones may also have been instruments providing information to the early sages about earthly meas-
urements and celestial events such as planetary conjunctions,
phases of the moon, solar eclipses and other lore needed to maintain
tribal life in harmony with the cosmic matrix.

Classical authors commented that "the belief in Pythagoras is
strong among the . . . [Celts, who taught] that the souls of men are

---

[166] Dames, *Mythic Ireland*, p. 215.
[167] Christopher Chippindale, quoted in Gordon Strachan, *Jesus the Master
Builder: Druid Mysteries and the Dawn of Christianity*, p. 217.
[168] See Martin Brennan, *The Boyne Valley Vision*.

immortal."[169] I think that the strength of belief goes beyond immortality to include a whole proto-Pythagorean cosmology that we can see is expressed in the figure of the Dagda himself. The temple builders of Neolithic Ireland were concerned with the direct contemplation of cosmic principles. They sought and created experiences that provide contact with a divine reality seen to be immanent throughout the cosmos and manifest in the world of physical phenomena.

In the Pythagorean system, which grew out of this earlier cosmology, numbers are divine, universal, qualitative principles that constitute the basic proportions and structure of order. One of the Dagda's names, "*Scotbe*," may translate as "Reckoner." In mythology his role includes the definitions of reckoning as laid out in the *Oxford English Dictionary:* "to enumerate serially or separately, to name or mention one after the another or in due order . . . to count so as to ascertain the number or amount of." Perhaps this name also suggests his knowledge of number and the role it plays in computation and ordering. Certainly he represents the four aspects through which divine numbers revealed themselves to the Pythagoreans. For them number in itself was arithmetic. Number in space was geometry and, hence, architecture. Number in time was music or harmonic resonance and attunement. Number in space-time was astronomy-astrology. Taken together, they make up a system of knowledge seeking the harmonious correspondences that existed between the different disciplines, humankind, and the cosmos.[170]

A modern Scots writer, Gordon Strachan, explains that for the Pythagoreans:

> The cosmos above was the macrocosmic universe. The cosmos below was the microcosmic individual. Between these was the mesocosm, the middle world, the third term, the mean proportional, spatially understood. This was the sacred space, the temenos, the tem-

---

[169] Ammianus Marcellinus, quoted in Kock and Carey, eds., *The Celtic Heroic Age*, p. 25.
[170] Guthrie, ed. and trans., *Pythagorean Sourcebook*, pp. 34ff.

ple, the special site where macrocosmic energies could be focused and mediated to microcosmic men and women, tuning them to the divine. Understood according to this cosmology, the stone circles [and other megalithic architecture] would have been centres where these divine energies could have been experienced . . . . Every number and geometric shape was assumed to correspond to a divine principle, active in the macrocosm and accessible in these sacred enclosures, so long as they exactly embodied the right numbers, proportions, and shapes. These principles were held to be the basis of music, the music of the heavenly spheres and human music as its earthly counterpart. Thus the astronomical alignments . . . would not only have been used for seasonal farming, fishing and sailing purposes. They would also have been considered as alignments to, and transmitters of, the energies of the gods and goddesses who were themselves often identified with the heavenly bodies. It was thus of utmost importance to keep in tune with them in order to predict what fate they had in store.[171]

The Pythagoreans believed that while number is the source and root of all things, "Unity is the dominant principle underlying number. In other words [they] did not see One as a number at all, but rather as the immutable principle that underlies all reckoning."[172]

Since number and tone are translatable into geometric imagery, this unity is revealed in the primary geometric image of the circle. Unity and circle are also embodied in the notion of the cycle as numerical series expressed via multiplication and division, and in harmonic octaves and intervals.[173] Unity is also expressed in the Neolithic stone temple mounds, in the endlessly rotating succession of the seasons harped by the Dagda, and in the revolutions of the starry heavens with which the Dagda's temples are aligned. From this perspective, the god's name, "Wheel," takes on a deeper and awesome meaning. And we can feel its resonance with two others

---

[171] *Jesus the Master Builder*, p. 218.

[172] Theon of Smyrna, quoted in Guthrie, ed. and trans., *Pythagorean Sourcebook*, p. 21.

[173] Ibid., pp. 20ff.

that the goddess chanted: "Existence (or Being)," and "Regeneration of the World."

All of this evidence suggests to me that the tales clearly allude to the cosmic dimensions of the old god. In spite of later detractors, the texts themselves and what they refer to in the landscape reveal his original glory. He represents the sacred geometer and master builder, musician, magus, sage ruler and cosmologist, embodying pre-Pythagorean wisdom. Appreciation of such totality is conveyed through created images of an immense, interrelated order as well as through his corporeal abundance and capacity to hold polarities in equilibrium.

Perhaps the Dagda is the earliest named figure in Europe representing the sacred tradition that endured through the millennia and was incorporated into the architecture of the great cathedrals of Europe. Chartres, a Gothic marvel that contains profound secrets of this tradition, was itself built in the land of the Carnutes, the site where Caesar tells us the druids held their great pan-Celtic assemblies.[174] At the cathedral school of Chartres during the twelfth century, there was also a singular and "brief and beautiful Renaissance of Pythagorean thought . . . due *in part* to a Latin translation of Plato's *Timaeus.*"[175]

The aspect of the Dagda that mediates cosmic order into culture and integrates individual identity with totality still comes through today in psychological material. It often manifests when the archetypal dimension opens through a profound wound in the personal parent-child complex that has skewed individual development. This opening usually occurs after consciousness is strong enough to begin to assimilate its immense potential. And with its perspective, we can begin to contemplate the meaning of our wounds. Rather than being identified with them, we can see that they open like tec-

---

[174] Louis Charpentier, *The Mysteries of Chartres Cathedral*, pp. 23ff.

[175] Guthrie, ed. and trans., *Pythagorean Sourcebook*, p. 43 (emphasis added). See also Charpentier, *Mysteries of Chartres Cathedral*, for a fuller discussion of the cathedral itself.

tonic plates to show what is beyond them—archetypal energies and forms that we have been destined to encounter in personal life, and sometimes beyond these, intimations of integration and even cosmic unity.

To give an example: after an eruption of rage, one client drew a picture of himself with a wound in his heart. He associated this wound to experiences of his father's abandonment of him. When we had worked on his anger and hurt and explored these emotions in our therapeutic relationship, he imaged the wound again and made another picture. This time he drew just the wounded heart with a hole and finally filled the void with an image of a man's head surrounded by stars. The night after the drawing he dreamt:

> I am looking at the man's face—the man from the drawing. It is green and like a giant, huge, alive, with a radiance that is really something—even has rays like a kind of halo over his ears. He seems totally accepting, as if he has seen everything.

In his personal associations to the head, the dreamer said the face reminded him of a man who claimed authority well in his work. And he added, "I don't. I've always been more ready to be angry at authority than to claim it." We can readily see the congruence of the archetypal and personal material. The archetypal image manifests through the wound to provide the potential to radically restructure the ego complex itself. The image shifts the father imago from the personally-experienced, rage-inducing betrayer to include the latent potentials of the archetypal level. While he had found some of this in the transference, the created/discovered image placed the potential in the center of his own heart, bridging the suprapersonal into his personal feeling life to provide a new way to father his own existence.[176] Such archetypal images usually occur in therapy at the opening of a new level of transformation and provide focus for further work. They seem to foreshadow and often

---

[176] Both this and the next figure were made green in the dream images, suggesting new life potentials arising to transform the wounded masculine.

support the process by which consciousness suffers through the constellated complex to touch and be expanded by the archetypal pattern at its core.

A similar example came in the drawing of the woman who dreamt of the bum on the bus, discussed earlier (above, page 50). It was done when she was in the throes of another phase of transformation in her animus. Thrown into primal terror that plunged her into the depths of her father complex, she encountered the terrible, judging Jehovah at her Ph.D. orals and, against all her expectations, survived and passed with distinction. Shaken by an encounter that she said felt "like the Inquisition," she made a drawing. It was a revelation of the shape-shifter Horned God as tree, animal, head and flaming menorah all combined. The night after she made the drawing, she also dreamed of it. In the dream, a figure bearing the drawn image as his own head carried under his arm came toward her across a three-span bridge. He also carried a lamp—a new mode of consciousness and guidance for her.

This figure is like the horned god, a transcendent, ever-living cosmic and chthonic power. Like the Green Knight Gawain encountered, he is able to let his head be cut off to start the new cycle, for he represents the ever-renewed life of nature, the ever-reborn consort of the Great Goddess. His figure comes toward the dreamer from the other side as a psychopomp with new wisdom—well beyond the previous sadistic judgmentalism of her animus.[177]

As the man's dream became a drawing, her drawing was immediately picked up in a dream image where its psychological context was enlarged. Such parallel manifestation in both outer and inner worlds is part of the borderland quality of the horned deity. As both a chthonic and cosmic deity never fully separated from the deep matrix of life, this figure acts as a harmonic bridge that permeates the area between the opposites. When this Dagda-like figure appears, material from both directions can be mediated to consciousness. Thus it functions just as the preverbal forms of music and

---

[177] See Perera, "Samain and Self."

proprioceptive awareness do: to permit us to experience the numinosity of archetypal energies underlying both affect and image. This area Jung named psychoid, and he defined it as the original unity of matter and spirit. Encountering it, we sense the numinous qualities that we associate with the Self and the godhead.

The horned deity is the guardian at the crossover, presenting what is to be faced and assimilated before the individual can enter the next stage of development. Not surprisingly, the horned Dagda image often appears as a representative of our core, and thus in conjunction with somatic symptoms. To give an example: a brilliant physicist and musician, very identified with intellectual and aesthetic elitism, repudiated aspects of the earthier masculine that his mother had openly scorned in his father. He dreamt:

> A big burly man, like a Paul Bunyan woodcutter, is letting off steam, cussing at a boys' camp (where boys learn to rough it and be close to nature). He's enjoying himself making all that noise. I feel oddly like hugging him, but I am shy. Also it would be impolite, unseemly, certainly nothing I would do with my father. I start to back away but he seems to know my hidden impulse and gives me a bear hug around my neck. I look up at him. He's huge and has his hair or something weirdly curled over his ears. I feel afraid, but I know that I am in his service now.

Associating to the giant figure, the dreamer said, "He is crude, coarse, not my type, not precise and intellectual at all, but at home in nature." To his sense of shyness and fear in the dream, he associated his telling me that he had told his wife to shut up, and he had been uncomfortable about "revealing that he could be such a brute."

He not only considered the remark "too rough and uncouth," but its revelation had given him a somatic symptom—activating the psychoid level where matter and psyche are still one. He developed a pain in the neck during the night of the dream, just where the giant hugged him. His proud neck and his identification with intellect and gentility were now gripped by another energy. In astrology we learn that Taurus, the sign of the bull, rules the neck.

I took the dream to imply that his psyche was challenging therapy to be a good-enough boys' camp where he could "learn to rough it and be close to nature." He consciously held an ideal of analysis as a "proper school" where he could participate intellectually and where he felt he should behave according to the standards of his "polite mother." The burly figure in the dream thus represents potential aspects of masculinity that deeply threatened his previous sense of identity. We can also recall that the giant woodsman Paul Bunyan had a great ox named Babe. Hence he is an American folk version of the bull god.

9

A Model for Male Development

All things must transform and only that which transforms remains true.
—Jung, *Mysterium Coniunctionis.*[178]

The Dagda as Father

Good at everything, passionate and wise, the Dagda is called "Great Father" and "Father of All." He is also the father of certain gods. In some texts he is said to be the father of Ogma, the figure representing both the force of poetry and physical strength, two aspects of power that the Irish valued equally. He also sires Dian Cecht, god of healing. Knowing his own fullness, we can see that these functions are his to bestow. In some texts, he is said to be the father of the three Brigids, although it is probable that the triple goddess named Brigid is his coequal and wife, sister or mother. By giving him a paternal role, however, the scribes who wrote down the old tales were supporting a cultural shift they favored. It is one similar to, but less extreme than the one that developed in Mediterranean areas. In Greece, Zeus's possessive assaults on his many paramours image a brutal takeover by people worshipping a sky god of lands held by the earlier goddess-worshipping tribes.

Unlike the father gods of many cultures, the Dagda is remarkably loving toward his children. For one daughter he creates a magical washtub.[179] It leaks at high tide, providing a gift of flexibility that all of us need. This special cleaning vessel functions to keep us adequately contained within the permeable borders that the god of boundaries sanctions. When the waters of unconsciousness rise

---

[178] Par. 503. I have changed the translation from "change" to "transform," which Edward C. Whitmont felt is closer to the original German (personal communication).

[179] Her name, Ainge, may refer to sow. She may be a deity of fertility, the ebb and flow of waters, and owner of a version of the vessel of inspiration.

with the fullness of life's inevitable rhythmic flowing, the created vessel leaks to excrete what might threaten us with flooding. We can see this as the generous deity's created capacity for our cups to run over into art or any other culturally valued expression, rather than to pressure us with emotionality or eruptive passions that would overwhelm us. It is an image for the gift of a creative and flexible consciousness.

We know a snippet of a late story in which the Dagda carries a wounded son all over the world to find healing. When another son is killed, he weeps tears of blood.[180] He helps a third to find the beloved he met in a dream. We know too that he turned to that same Angus, the Mac Oc (his son with Boann), to give him advice and help in his indentured service and starvation. He respects his son and the younger man's different kind of wisdom, for he is willing to learn in order to support the life process. He even lets himself be dispossessed by this son, who uses a riddle to assert his claim.

As a truly generous and just father securely bonded with his son, the Dagda gives up his own dwelling to the young god. Like the human fathers who let their children win at games to support their growing confidence and to model the graceful acceptance of defeat, he accepts limitation and steps aside. He lets his son win his own domain. He does not require that his son remain subservient to paternal authority as our patrifocal system requires. Instead he contributes paternal libido to empower the next generation, thereby supporting the life process and a future that could grow beyond himself—very unlike Cuchullain who fought and killed his heroic boy to honor himself and the men of Ulster.

In this story, the Dagda as chief of the gods allots the underground temples or *sid* mounds of Ireland to his tribe. Finally his son Angus the Mac Oc arrives and asks for his share, a place of his own.

---

[180] Gray, *Cath Maige Tuired,* p. 121.

"I have none for thee," said the Dagda, "I have completed the division."

"Then let me be granted . . . a day and a night in thy own dwelling." That was given to him.

"Go now to thy following," said the Dagda [the next day], "since thou hast consumed thy time."

"It is clear," said the Mac Oc, "that night and day are the whole world, and it is that which has been given to me."

Thereupon the Dagda went out and the Mac Oc remained in his [father's] *sid*.[181]

The Mac Oc explains this riddle in another tale that takes us both back to proto-Pythagorean cosmology and ahead to chaos theory. (And we can see in the art of both how similar are the forms that express them if we compare the Neolithic and La Tene styles' multispiral forms with illustrations of the Mandelbrot Set.) The youth says, "It is in days and nights that the world is spent."[182] Through similarity of form, the cycle of day and night is a microcosm containing the whole macrocosmic cycle of time. Each moment, day or year thus stands for and is transfused with the significance of the whole in mystic thinking and in both ancient and modern mathematics. The present cycle stands for all time. Through similarity of form, every instance stands for the whole. Thus the Celts related every hill and kingly mound to the hill of the high king at Tara, every water source to the well of truth and wisdom.

We readily experience this *pars pro toto* in childhood, in the grip of our complexes, and in regressive states. Experience of this correlation can sometimes be acquired in meditation. Then each concrete and particular experience of reality can be felt as part of a hologram, a symbolic manifestation of an interrelated whole. From this perspective, the landscape of our days becomes filled with symbolic significance, each event penetrated by the sacred. The

---

181 From "The Book of Leinster," quoted in Rees and Rees, *Celtic Heritage*, p. 88.
182 "The Wooing of Etain," ibid.

capacity to focus through microcosmic particulars to what we now call the archetypal, implicate order was so obvious to early, pre-Celtic consciousness that the Dagda easily submits to his own dispossession.

The fact that the day and night of the son's tenancy are the day and night of Samain adds another dimension. This date represents a critical moment when transformative energies can emerge, for Samain—our Hallowe'en—is one of the cracks between the summer and winter year. At this time, nature and the supernatural are in particularly open interchange. Thus, one king can depart while another emerges. The tale of the Mac Oc's peaceful takeover may express a cultural antecedent to the later, Bronze Age rites of changeover of mythic Celtic rulers, which also took place at Samain. These involve the old king's death by stabbing, strangling, burning, drowning, or all of these.

In the older story of transformation, the Dagda models a willing acceptance of change and a sacrifice made out of personal connection to his son and knowledge of the archetypal matrix of life. It involves his generosity to let the son of the goddess claim the place he had ruled—the goddess's great mound of Newgrange. The early Celtic god did not step outside of his secure relationship to the goddess. Unlike the radically separated individuals we seek to become, he and the tribal society he represented knew they belonged within the pattern and processes of that deep matrix. Thus in ancient cultures, death and endings had a very different flavor than they generally have today.

Beyond that, this sacrifice of the father for the son reminds us that we, who so value our individuality, may now need a perspective based in consciousness of our larger life matrix. With change, the psychological homes we cherish and identify with are inevitably taken from us, or they lose their significance. Looking to the macrocosmic, symbolic patterns behind the values to which we cling may make us better able to surrender to their endings. Like the Dagda, we may then tune into the overarching process and wisely see its interconnections. With love and respect for the new life, we can, perhaps, make way for the young son of the ever-young goddess of the great whole, and accept the many deaths that ongoing life systems require.

When we have worked through the narcissistic wounds to our self-esteem so we are full enough to be in touch with our true Self, we can give up control and one-sided, heroic striving. Then we may accept our limited place in the whole, even as we feel how intimately we participate in its vastness. From this security we can almost willingly make space for what will inevitably dispossess us. This seems critical in the contemporary world if we are to move beyond our warlike needs for ever-expanding conquest, colonization and consumption.

Our ancient ancestors were still ruled by reverence for the cycle of life in which they participated and felt held. For them the right and power of the father god was not always supreme over the son as it becomes in later Celtic and Christian mythology. Son succeeds father, as king succeeds king, and the dispossessed or dying one returns to the goddess in the other world to become a protective wisdom figure (like the figures of Bran, Arthur, Merlin). At each stage the young son, youthful warrior, partner/king, and initiated wisdom figure remain related to the goddess. The young male is not required to separate and stand as adversary against mother, earth and his own chthonic nature. He does not have to kill off a dragon, to suppress and conquer the feminine, and later reclaim her as possession, wife and muse. Human beings and consciousness develop in relationship to teachers of both genders. This implies a more balanced, ever-expanding maturation supported through all the stages of physical, emotional, intellectual and social growth. Within the bonds of family and social group, the evolving individual learns, strengthens, differentiates and tests identity and strengths with and against others. When ready, the youth replaces the previous authority to become initiated as another temporary, adult partner of the goddess of process to father a new generation.

As we have seen with the Dagda, the figure in this partnership phase engenders and cares for the very forms that will dispossess it.

Growing beyond phallic aggressiveness and the youthful hero to accept the role of regal authority, the partner rules in accord with the demands of the matrix of being, honoring all phases of development. This entails ordering inner and outer diversity in a manner that serves life. It also entails learning to wisely and generously sustain relationships and find a metaperspective to justly manage what would be oppositions in the warrior phase. The capacity for encompassing, ordering and surrendering, rather than polarizing, brings inner conflict and suffering, as well as richness, spaciousness and depth. It supports increasing complexity and the expression of a full range of affects and forms of consciousness.

Since each stage of development occurs in relation to the feminine—as womb, nurturer and initiatrix, as partner, and as death—individual identity is not only localized in a particular time and space, it endures through the whole life cycle and the ever-reshaping energies within it. Transcending the momentary and small scale, the individual gains awareness of the wheel of time itself, the rotating seasons and the starry heavens. Thus becoming a magus, with consciousness permeable to a larger processual scale, the individual attunes with and participates in the hologram shared with all forms of life.

The grandeur of the Dagda offers us a perspective to refocus and enlarge our sense of what masculinity could be. We can see that his attunement with relational, flowing process has a very different quality than it holds in patrifocal models. The cycles are linked with ongoing biological processes that are akin to the stages of classical female development—the maturation from child to maiden to maternal creator and caretaker to crone. Such a relational, matrix-based process of change suggests an open, self-organizing system that moves through inevitable chaotic phases in an ever-unfolding complexity.

While I will not go deeply here into the ramifications of this model, I feel it points us to a paradigm of male development that is especially useful today. It also provides a way of thinking about the many similarly structured, smaller scale and isomorphic phases of personal development that we suffer throughout the processes of life-long individuation.

With this holistic view, we can more readily accept that we are both singular and multiform throughout our development. We can learn to endure the transitional passages with less anxiety. We may even abide and nurture each disorganization we are given to suffer until its new patterns become clearer and even meaningful. Attuned to and bonded in the overarching archetypal process, we can then perhaps more gracefully sacrifice our currently held sense of identity, and find the security to submit to inevitable phases of unknowing and move through them.

The painful side of the ongoing relationship to the matrix of transformation is our mistrust and fear. We are not the Dagda. Often we are without the adequate early experiences that might instill trust. The unknown may seem to be only another danger, threatening loss of control, abandonment and/or engulfment. Such terrors arouse our defenses and our power shadow. Thus we assume an adversarial stance. Fighting our own development, we identify with the youthful hero's desire for control and domination. We refuse the many invitations we receive to soften, open and grow. Instead we hunker down to hold onto what we think is safe. Thus we remain embedded in regressive, defensive positions, or flee into the many forms of addiction to avoid the challenges of development.

This dynamic, both in society and in ourselves, motivates fundamentalism and the repudiation of anything new. These defensive attitudes rekindle desires that belong to previous developmental phases and tempt us to serve outmoded ideals rather than risk taking the next step in the ongoing life process. Without dealing with our fear, without the Dagda's assurance of flexibility and some access to his divine gusto, we are thereby destined to live narrowly, not transformationally.

The image of the Dagda may stand as a beacon on the journey that leads through fearful transitions to the growth of consciousness. He bridges two tribes and integrates the structures of several epochs. He can defend when necessary or be actively receptive when required. His capacity to order is flexible and in accord with the requirements of the goddesses of the life process whom he loves and serves. He stands respectfully and firmly confident of his equality with them. Secure in his physical and spiritual power and his ability to play creatively with the range of emotions, he recognizes the joys of relationship that allow creative, mutual appreciation. He is a potent and wonderful image of integrated masculine fullness and depth that might lead us out of the defensive, simplistic factionalism in which so much of the world still cowers.

Conclusion

In the Dagda we have a figure that is powerful, active and receptive. Creative lord of life and death, maker and crosser of boundaries, he expresses the fullness and paradoxical nature of being. Both chthonic and spiritual, he assists us to move toward the full capacities of consciousness to integrate nonverbal, symbolic, rational and mystical ways of perceiving and processing information.

He embodies a primal wholeness that vividly encompasses some of the mutually dependent polarities that humans are consciously struggling with today: life and death, nurturance and war, containment and rejection, creativity and destruction, ugliness and beauty, chaos and order, wisdom and ineptitude, male and female, receptivity and aggression, grief and comedy, refined sensitivity and lusty coarseness, ruling and submitting, abundance and deprivation, spiritual enlightenment and chthonic power.

This image of paradoxical unity enables us to accept a very wide range of experiences. It supports our wholeness by avoiding an overdependence on rationality. It encourages alogical, lateral, and "all-round" thinking as we move around in the clusters of these attributes.[183] It affirms many kinds of interrelating energy patterns. As a divine ancestor beckoning us across more than seven thousand

---

[183] See "Psychology and Religion," *Psychology and Religion,* CW 11, par. 159, note 59; cf. Edward F. Edinger, *The Mysterium Lectures: A Journey through C.G. Jung's* Mysterium Coniunctionis, p. 20.

years of history and even across species, the image of the Dagda helps us to expand our consciousness of what wholeness in both genders can mean.

As Jung puts it, coming from the modern rational perspective:

> A paradoxical God-image forces [us] to come to grips with [our] own paradoxicality [and, as he says repeatedly, our wholeness]. That is in fact our task which we have hitherto avoided.[184]

So, as we put our shoulders to the great wheel and struggle to reintegrate what is unitary before and beyond the paradoxes, we may both retrieve and welcome our potential for an authentic, full life. Perhaps we can even "arrive where we started" and, full of the experiences of our many transformations, begin truly to "know the place for the first time."

---

[184] *Letters,* vol. 2, p. 102.

Bibliography

Brennan, Martin. *The Boyne Valley Vision*. Portlaoise, Ireland: Dolmen Press, 1980.

Bromwich, Rachel, ed. and trans. *Trioedd Ynys Prydein: The Welsh Triads*. Cardiff: University of Wales, 1961.

Buruma, Ian, and Margalit, Avishai. "Occidentalism." In *The New York Review of Books,* vol. XLIX, no. 1 (Jan. 17, 2000).

Charpentier, Louis. *The Mysteries of Chartres Cathedral*. New York: Avon, 1972.

Chevalier, Jean, et al. *The Penguin Dictionary of Symbols*. London: Penguin, 1969.

Conforti, Michael. *Field, Form and Fate: Patterns in Mind, Nature and Psyche*. Woodstock, CT: Spring Publications, 1999.

Cowen, R. "Sounds of the Universe Confirm the Big Bang." In *Science News,* vol. 159 (April 28, 2001).

Dames, Michael. *Mythic Ireland*. London: Thames and Hudson, 1992.

Dumezil, Georges. *Gods of the Ancient Northmen*. Berkeley, CA: University of California Press, 1974.

Edinger, Edward F. *Ego and Archetype: Individuation and the Religious Function of the Psyche*. Boston: Shambhala, 1992.

_____. *The Mysterium Lectures: A Journey through C.G. Jung's Mysterium Coniunctionis*. Toronto: Inner City Books, 1995.

Eliot, T.S. *Four Quartets*. London: Faber and Faber, 1944.

Ford, Patrick K. "Aspects of the Patrician Legend." In *Celtic Folklore and Christianity*. Ed. Patrick K. Ford. Santa Barbara, CA: McNally and Loftin, 1983.

Gantz, Jeffrey, trans. and ed. *Early Irish Myths and Sagas*. New York: Penguin, 1981.

_____. *The Mabinogion*. New York: Penguin, 1976.

Gebser, Jean. *The Ever-Present Origin.* Trans. Noel Barstad and Algis Mickunas. Athens, OH: Ohio University Press, 1985.

Germano, Donna. *Women and the Tears of Men.* Private printing.

Gimbutas, Marija, *The Goddesses and Gods of Old Europe: Myths and Cult Images.* Berkeley: University of California Press, 1982.

Girard, Rene. *Violence and the Sacred.* Trans. Patrick Gregory. Baltimore: Johns Hopkins, 1977.

Gray, Elizabeth A., ed. *Cath Maige Tuired: The Second Battle of Mag Tuired.* London: Irish Texts Society, vol. 52, 1983.

Guthrie, Kenneth Sylvan, ed. and trans. *The Pythagorean Sourcebook and Library.* Grand Rapids, MI: Phanes Press, 1987.

Gwynn, E., ed. *The Metrical Dindschenchas.* Dublin: School of Celtic Studies, 1924.

Haddon, Genia. *Uniting Sex, Self and Spirit.* Private printing.

Hall, Edward T. *The Dance of Life: The Other Dimension of Time.* New York: Anchor Books, 1984.

Herrigel, Eugen. *Zen in the Art of Archery.* New York: Vintage, 1971.

Ives, Colta, and Stein, Susan. *The Lure of the Exotic: Gauguin in New York Collections.* New York: Metropolitan Musum, 2000.

Jeffares, A. Norman, ed. *W.B. Yeats: Selected Poetry.* London: MacMillan, 1962.

Jenks, Tom. "Where Are the Men?" In *The San Francisco Jung Institute Library Journal,* vol. 20, no. 3 (2001).

Jobes, Gertrude, ed. *Dictionary of Mythology, Folklore and Symbols.* New York. Scarecrow Press, 1961.

Jung, C.G. *The Collected Works* (Bollingen Series XX). 20 vols. Trans. R.F.C. Hull, Ed. H. Read, M. Fordham, G. Adler, Wm. McGuire. Princeton: Princeton University Press, 1953-1979.

_____. *Letters* (Bollingen Series XCV). 2 vols. Ed. Gerhard Adler and Aniela Jaffé. Princeton: Princeton University Press, 1973.

_____. *Dream Analysis: Notes of the Seminar Given in 1928-1930* (Bollingen Series XCIX). Ed. William McGuire. Princeton: Princeton University Press, 1984.

Kalsched, Donald. *The Inner World of Trauma: Archetypal Defenses of the Personal Spirit.* New York: Routledge, 1996.

Khan, M. Inayat. "Abstract Sound." In *Heart and Wings,* Winter-Spring 2002.

Kinsella, Thomas, ed. and trans. *The Tain (Tain Bo Cuailnge).* Oxford: Oxford University Press, 1970.

Knoblauch, Steven. *The Musical Edge of Therapeutic Dialogue.* Hillsdale, NJ: The Analytic Press, 2000.

Koch, John, and Carey, John, eds. *The Celtic Heroic Age: Literary Sources for Ancient Celtic Europe and Early Ireland and Wales.* Malden, MA: Celtic Studies, 1995.

Lake, Nell. "Cortices in C Minor." In *Harvard Magazine,* March-April 2002.

Leroi-Gourhan, André. *Treasures of Prehistoric Art.* New York: Harry N. Abrams, 1980.

MacNeill, Maire. *The Festival of Lughnasa: A Study of the Survival of the Celtic Festival of the Beginning of Harvest.* Oxford: Oxford University Press, 1962.

McClain, Ernest G. *The Pythagorean Plato: Prelude to the Song Itself.* York Beach, ME: Nicolas-Hays, 1978.

McCort, Frank. *Angela's Ashes.* New York: Scribners, 1996.

Markale, Jean. *Celtic Civilization.* London: Gordon and Cremonesi, 1976.

Montague, John. *John Montague: Collected Poems.* Winston-Salem: Wake Forest, 1995.

Newell, Martha Mae. "Sounding Through the Mask: The Person and Sound." In *Quadrant,* vol. 30, no. 1 (Winter 2000).

North, John. *Stonehenge: Neolithic Man and the Cosmos.* London: Harper Collins, 1996.

O'Driscoll, Robert, ed. *The Celtic Consciousness.* New York: George Braziller, 1981.

O hOgian, Daithi. *Myth, Legend and Romance: Encyclopedia of the Irish Folk Tradition.* London: Ryan, 1990.

_____. *The Sacred Isle: Belief and Religion in Pre-Christian Ireland.* Cork: Collins, 1999.

Perera, Sylvia Brinton. *Descent to the Goddess: A Way of Initiation for Women.* Toronto: Inner City Books, 1981.

_____. *The Scapegoat Complex: Toward a Mythology of Shadow and Guilt.* Toronto: Inner City Books, 1986.

_____. "Ritual Integration of Aggression in Psychotherapy." In *The Borderline Personality in Analysis.* Ed. Nathan Schwartz-Salant and Murray Stein. Wilmette, IL: Chiron, 1988.

_____. "War, Madness, and the Morrigan: A Celtic Goddess of Life and Death." In *Mad Parts of Sane People in Analysis.* Ed. Murray Stein. Wilmette, IL: Chiron, 1993.

_____. "Samain and Self: Uncanny Images of Transformation." In *Text of Papers Presented at the 1996 National Conference of Jungian Analysis.* New York, 1996.

_____. *Celtic Queen Maeve and Addiction: An Archetypal Perspective.* York Beach, ME: Nicolas-Hays, 2001.

Rees, Alwyn, and Rees, Brinley. *Celtic Heritage: Ancient Tradition in Ireland and Wales.* London: Thames and Hudson, 1961.

Ross, Anne. *Pagan Celtic Britain: Studies in Iconography and Tradition.* London: Routledge and Kegan Paul, 1967.

Sheldrake, Rupert. *Dogs That Know When Their Owners Are Coming Home: And Other Unexplained Powers of Animals.* New York: Three Rivers Press, 1999.

Sjoestedt, Marie-Louise. *Gods and Heroes of the Celts.* Berkeley, CA: Turtle Island, 1982.

Stewart, R.J. *Music and the Elemental Psyche.* Rochester, VT: Destiny Books, 1987.

Strachan, Gordon. *Jesus the Master Builder: Druid Mysteries and the Dawn of Christianity.* Edinburgh: Floris, 1998.

Volk, Jeff, ed. *Of Sound Mind and Body: Music and Vibrational Healing.* Video. Epping, NH: Lumina Productions, 1992.

Whitlock, Ralph. *In Search of Lost Gods: A Guide to British Folklore.* Oxford: Phaidon, 1979.

Whitmont, Edward. C. *The Symbolic Quest: Basic Concepts of Analytical Psychology.* Princeton: Princeton University Press, 1991.

_____. *The Alchemy of Healing: Psyche and Soma.* Berkeley, CA: North Atlantic Books, 1993.

Wilber, Ken *Integral Psychology: Consciousness, Spirit, Psychology, Therapy.* Boston: Shambhala Publications, 2002.

Index

Page nos. in *italic* refer to illustrations

Studies in Jungian Psychology
by Jungian Analysts

Quality Paperbacks

Prices and payment in $US (except in Canada, $Cdn)

1. The Secret Raven: Conflict and Transformation
Daryl Sharp (Toronto). ISBN 0-919123-00-7. 128 pp. $16

2. The Psychological Meaning of Redemption Motifs in Fairy Tales
Marie-Louise von Franz (Zürich). ISBN 0-919123-01-5. 128 pp. $16

3. On Divination and Synchronicity: The Psychology of Meaningful Chance
Marie-Louise von Franz (Zürich). ISBN 0-919123-02-3. 128 pp. $16

4. The Owl Was a Baker's Daughter: Obesity, Anorexia and the Repressed Feminine Marion Woodman (Toronto). ISBN 0-919123-03-1. 144 pp. $18

5. Alchemy: An Introduction to the Symbolism and the Psychology
Marie-Louise von Franz (Zürich). ISBN 0-919123-04-X. 288 pp. $22

6. Descent to the Goddess: A Way of Initiation for Women
Sylvia Brinton Perera (New York). ISBN 0-919123-05-8. 112 pp. $16

8. Border Crossings: Carlos Castaneda's Path of Knowledge
Donald Lee Williams (Boulder). ISBN 0-919123-07-4. 160 pp. $18

9. Narcissism and Character Transformation: The Psychology of Narcissistic Character Disorders
Nathan Schwartz-Salant (New York). ISBN 0-919123-08-2. 192 pp. $20

11. Alcoholism and Women: The Background and the Psychology
Jan Bauer (Montreal). ISBN 0-919123-10-4. 144 pp. $18

12. Addiction to Perfection: The Still Unravished Bride
Marion Woodman (Toronto). ISBN 0-919123-11-2. 208 pp. $20pb/$25hc

13. Jungian Dream Interpretation: A Handbook of Theory and Practice
James A. Hall, M.D. (Dallas). ISBN 0-919123-12-0. 128 pp. $16

14. The Creation of Consciousness: Jung's Myth for Modern Man
Edward F. Edinger (Los Angeles). ISBN 0-919123-13-9. 128 pp. $16

15. The Analytic Encounter: Transference and Human Relationship
Mario Jacoby (Zürich). ISBN 0-919123-14-7. 128 pp. $16

16. Change of Life: Dreams and the Menopause
Ann Mankowitz (Ireland). ISBN 0-919123-15-5. 128 pp. $16

17. The Illness That We Are: A Jungian Critique of Christianity
John P. Dourley (Ottawa). ISBN 0-919123-16-3. 128 pp. $16

18. Hags and Heroes: A Feminist Approach to Jungian Psychotherapy with Couples Polly Young-Eisendrath (Philadelphia). ISBN 0-919123-17-1. 192 pp. $20

19. Cultural Attitudes in Psychological Perspective
Joseph L. Henderson, M.D. (San Francisco). ISBN 0-919123-18-X. 128 pp. $16

20. The Vertical Labyrinth: Individuation in Jungian Psychology
Aldo Carotenuto (Rome). ISBN 0-919123-19-8. 144 pp. $18

21. The Pregnant Virgin: A Process of Psychological Transformation
Marion Woodman (Toronto). ISBN 0-919123-20-1. 208 pp. $20pb/$25hc

22. Encounter with the Self: A Jungian Commentary on William Blake's
Illustrations of the Book of Job
Edward F. Edinger (Los Angeles). ISBN 0-919123-21-X. 80 pp. $16

23. The Scapegoat Complex: Toward a Mythology of Shadow and Guilt
Sylvia Brinton Perera (New York). ISBN 0-919123-22-8. 128 pp. $16

24. The Bible and the Psyche: Individuation Symbolism in the Old Testament
Edward F. Edinger (Los Angeles). ISBN 0-919123-23-6. 176 pp. $20

25. The Spiral Way: A Woman's Healing Journey
Aldo Carotenuto (Rome). ISBN 0-919123-24-4. 144 pp. $18

26. The Jungian Experience: Analysis and Individuation
James A. Hall, M.D. (Dallas). ISBN 0-919123-25-2. 176 pp. $20

27. Phallos: Sacred Image of the Masculine
Eugene Monick (Scranton, PA). ISBN 0-919123-26-0. 144 pp. $18

28. The Christian Archetype: A Jungian Commentary on the Life of Christ
Edward F. Edinger (Los Angeles). ISBN 0-919123-27-9. 144 pp. $18

29. Love, Celibacy and the Inner Marriage
John P. Dourley (Ottawa). ISBN 0-919123-28-7. 128 pp. $16

30. Touching: Body Therapy and Depth Psychology
Deldon Anne McNeely (Lynchburg, VA). ISBN 0-919123-29-5. 128 pp. $16

31. Personality Types: Jung's Model of Typology
Daryl Sharp (Toronto). ISBN 0-919123-30-9. 128 pp. $16

32. The Sacred Prostitute: Eternal Aspect of the Feminine
Nancy Qualls-Corbett (Birmingham). ISBN 0-919123-31-7. 176 pp. $20

33. When the Spirits Come Back
Janet O. Dallett (Seal Harbor, WA). ISBN 0-919123-32-5. 160 pp. $18

34. The Mother: Archetypal Image in Fairy Tales
Sibylle Birkhäuser-Oeri (Zürich). ISBN 0-919123-33-3. 176 pp. $20

35. The Survival Papers: Anatomy of a Midlife Crisis
Daryl Sharp (Toronto). ISBN 0-919123-34-1. 160 pp. $18

36. The Cassandra Complex: Living with Disbelief
Laurie Layton Schapira (New York). ISBN 0-919123-35-X. 160 pp. $18

37. Dear Gladys: The Survival Papers, Book 2
Daryl Sharp (Toronto). ISBN 0-919123-36-8. 144 pp. $18

39. Acrobats of the Gods: Dance and Transformation
Joan Dexter Blackmer (Wilmot Flat, NH). ISBN 0-919123-38-4. 128 pp. $16

40. Eros and Pathos: Shades of Love and Suffering
Aldo Carotenuto (Rome). ISBN 0-919123-39-2. 160 pp. $18

41. The Ravaged Bridegroom: Masculinity in Women
Marion Woodman (Toronto). ISBN 0-919123-42-2. 224 pp. $22

43. Goethe's *Faust:* Notes for a Jungian Commentary
Edward F. Edinger (Los Angeles). ISBN 0-919123-44-9. 112 pp. $16

44. The Dream Story: Everything You Wanted To Know
Donald Broadribb (Baker's Hill, Australia). ISBN 0-919123-45-7. 256 pp. $24

45. The Rainbow Serpent: Bridge to Consciousness
Robert L. Gardner (Toronto). ISBN 0-919123-46-5. 128 pp. $16

46. Circle of Care: Clinical Issues in Jungian Therapy
Warren Steinberg (New York). ISBN 0-919123-47-3. 160 pp. $18

71. **The Aion Lectures: Exploring the Self in C.G. Jung's** *Aion*
Edward F. Edinger (Los Angeles). ISBN 0-919123-72-4. 208 pp. $20

72. **Living Jung: The Good and the Better**
Daryl Sharp (Toronto). ISBN 0-919123-73-2. 128 pp. $16

73. **Swamplands of the Soul: New Life in Dismal Places**
James Hollis (Houston). ISBN 0-919123-74-0. 160 pp. $18

74. **Food and Transformation: Imagery and Symbolism of Eating**
Eve Jackson (London). ISBN 0-919123-75-9. 128 pp. $16

75. **Archetypes & Strange Attractors: The Chaotic World of Symbols**
John R. Van Eenwyk (Olympia, WA). ISBN 0-919123-76-7. 192 pp. $20

76. **Archetypal Patterns in Fairy Tales**
Marie-Louise von Franz (Zurich). ISBN 0-919123-77-5. 192 pp. $20

77. **C.G. Jung: His Myth in Our Time**
Marie-Louise von Franz (Zurich). ISBN 0-919123-78-3. 368 pp. $25

78. **Divine Tempest: The Hurricane As a Psychic Phenomenon**
David E. Schoen (New Orleans). ISBN 0-919123-79-1. 128 pp. $16

79. **The Eden Project: In Search of the Magical Other**
James Hollis (Houston). ISBN 0-919123-80-5. 160 pp. $18

80. **Jungian Psychology Unplugged: My Life As an Elephant**
Daryl Sharp (Toronto). ISBN 0-919123-81-3. 160 pp. $18

82. **Now or Neverland: Peter Pan and the Myth of Eternal Youth**
Ann Yeoman (Toronto). ISBN 0-919123-83-X. 192 pp. $20

83. **The Cat: A Tale of Feminine Redemption**
Marie-Louise von Franz (Zurich). ISBN 0-919123-84-8. 128 pp. $16

84. **Celebrating Soul: Preparing for the New Religion**
Lawrence W. Jaffe (Berkeley, CA). ISBN 0-919123-85-6. 128 pp. $16

85. **The Psyche in Antiquity, Book 1: Early Greek Philosophy**
Edward F. Edinger (Los Angeles). ISBN 0-919123-86-4. 128 pp. $16

86. **The Psyche in Antiquity, Book 2: Gnosticism and Early Christianity**
Edward F. Edinger (Los Angeles). ISBN 0-919123-87-2. 160 pp. $18

87. **The Problem of the Puer Aeternus**
Marie-Louise von Franz (Zurich). ISBN 0-919123-88-0. 288 pp. $22

88. **The Inner Journey: Lectures and Essays on Jungian Psychology**
Barbara Hannah (Zurich). ISBN 0-919123-89-9. 160 pp. $18

89. **Aurora Consurgens: A Document Attributed to Thomas Aquinas**
Commentary by Marie-Louise von Franz (Zurich). ISBN 0-919123-90-2. 576 pp. $40

90. **Ego and Self: The Old Testament Prophets**
Edward F. Edinger (Los Angeles). ISBN 0-919123-91-0. 160 pp. $18

91. **Visions in the Night: Jungian and Ancient Dream Interpretation**
Joel Covitz (Brookline, MA). ISBN 0-919123-92-9. 128 pp. $16

92. **Creating a Life: Finding Your Individual Path**
James Hollis (Houston). ISBN 0-919123-93-7. 160 pp. $18

93. **The Psyche on Stage: Individuation Motifs in Shakespeare and Sophocles**
Edward F. Edinger (Los Angeles). ISBN 0-919123-94-5. 96 pp. $16

94. **Jung and Yoga: The Psyche-Body Connection**
Judith Harris (London, Ontario). ISBN 0-919123-95-3. 160 pp. $18

95. Digesting Jung: Food for the Journey
Daryl Sharp (Toronto). ISBN 0-919123-96-1. 128 pp. $16

96. World Weary Woman: Her Wound and Transformation
Cara Barker (Kirkland, WA). ISBN 0-919123-97-X. 160 pp. $18

97. Animal Guides in Life, Myth and Dreams
Neil Russack (San Francisco). ISBN 0-919123-98-8. 224 pp. $22

98. The Complex: Path of Transformation from Archetype to Ego
Erel Shalit (Ra'anana, Israel). ISBN 0-919123-99-6. 128 pp. $16

**99. The Secret World of Drawings: A Jungian Approach
to Healing through Art**
Gregg M. Furth (New York). ISBN 1-894574-00-1. 176 pp. **100 illustrations** $20

100. Animus and Anima in Fairy Tales
Marie-Louise von Franz (Zurich). ISBN 1-894574-01-X. 128 pp. $16

101. Awakening Woman: Dreams and Individuation
Nancy Qualls-Corbett (Birmingham). ISBN 1-894574-02-8. 160 pp. $18

102. Science of the Soul: A Jungian Perspective
Edward F. Edinger (Los Angeles). ISBN 1-894574-03-6. 128 pp. $16

103. On This Journey We Call Our Life: Living the Questions
James Hollis (Houston). ISBN 1-894574-04-4. 160 pp. $18

**104.The Archetype of Renewal: Psychological Reflections on
the Aging, Death and Rebirth of the King**
D. Stephenson Bond (Boston). ISBN 1-894574-05-2. 160 pp. $16

105. Archetype Revisited: An Updated Natural History of the Self
Anthony Stevens (Corfu, Greece). ISBN 1-894574-06-0. 416 pp. $34

106. The Parental Image: Its Injury and Reconstruction
M. Esther Harding (New York). ISBN 1-894574-07-9. **3rd edition** 160 pp. $18

107. The Irish Bull God: Image of Multiform and Integral Masculinity
Sylvia Brinton Perera (New York). ISBN 1-894574-08-7. 160 pp. $18

108. The Sacred Psyche: A Psychological Approach to the Psalms
Edward F. Edinger (Los Angeles). ISBN 1-894574-09-5. 160 pp. $18

Discounts: any 3-5 books, 10%; 6-9 books, 20%; 10 or more, 25%
Add Postage/Handling: 1-2 books, $3 surface ($6 air); 3-4 books, $5 surface ($10 air);
5-9 books, $10 surface ($15 air); 10 or more, free surface ($20 air)

*Ask for **Jung at Heart** newsletter and **Complete Catalogue***

INNER CITY BOOKS
Box 1271, Station Q, Toronto, ON M4T 2P4, Canada

Tel. (416) 927-0355 / Fax (416) 924-1814 / E-mail: sales@innercitybooks.net